VALERIAN AND LAURELINE

AMBASSADOR OF THE SHADOWS

J.-C. MÉZIÈRES AND P. CHRISTIN
COLOUR WORK: E. TRANLÉ

9th CINEBOOK
The 9th Art Publisher

Original title: Valérian – L'Ambassadeur des Ombres

© 2016 Cinebook Ltd

Original edition: © Dargaud Paris, 1975 by Christin, Mézières & Tran-Lê
www.dargaud.com

English translation: © 2013 Cinebook Ltd

Translator: Jerome Saincantin
Lettering and text layout: Design Amorandi
Printed in France by PPO Graphic, 91120 Palaiseau

This edition first published in Great Britain in 2013 by
Cinebook Ltd
56 Beech Avenue
Canterbury, Kent
CT4 7TA
www.cinebook.com

A CIP catalogue record for this book
is available from the British Library

ISBN 978-1-84918-325-3

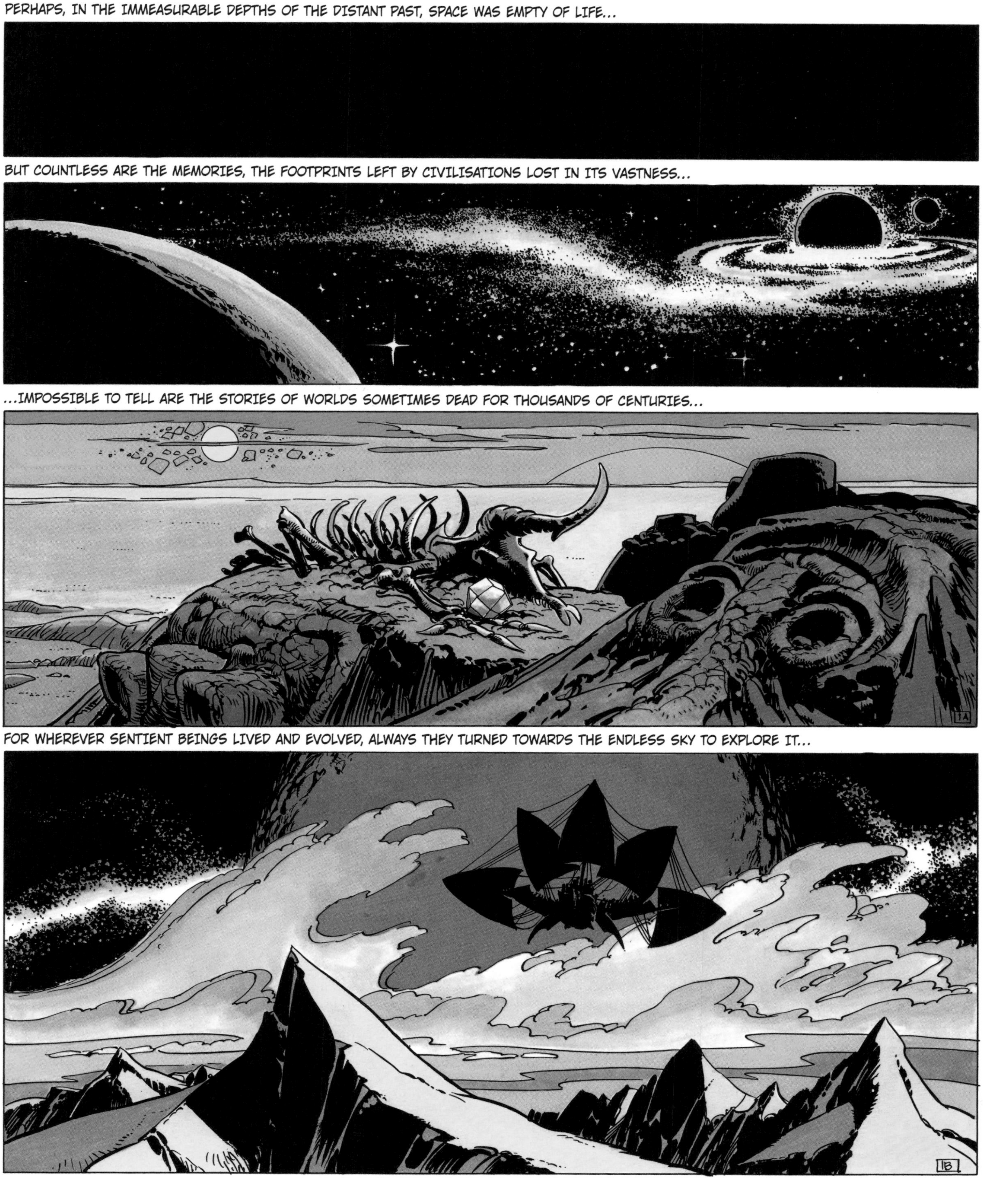
PERHAPS, IN THE IMMEASURABLE DEPTHS OF THE DISTANT PAST, SPACE WAS EMPTY OF LIFE...
BUT COUNTLESS ARE THE MEMORIES, THE FOOTPRINTS LEFT BY CIVILISATIONS LOST IN ITS VASTNESS...
...IMPOSSIBLE TO TELL ARE THE STORIES OF WORLDS SOMETIMES DEAD FOR THOUSANDS OF CENTURIES...
FOR WHEREVER SENTIENT BEINGS LIVED AND EVOLVED, ALWAYS THEY TURNED TOWARDS THE ENDLESS SKY TO EXPLORE IT...

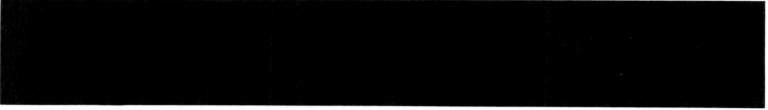

MANY AIMLESS QUESTS ENDED WITH NO ENCOUNTERS...

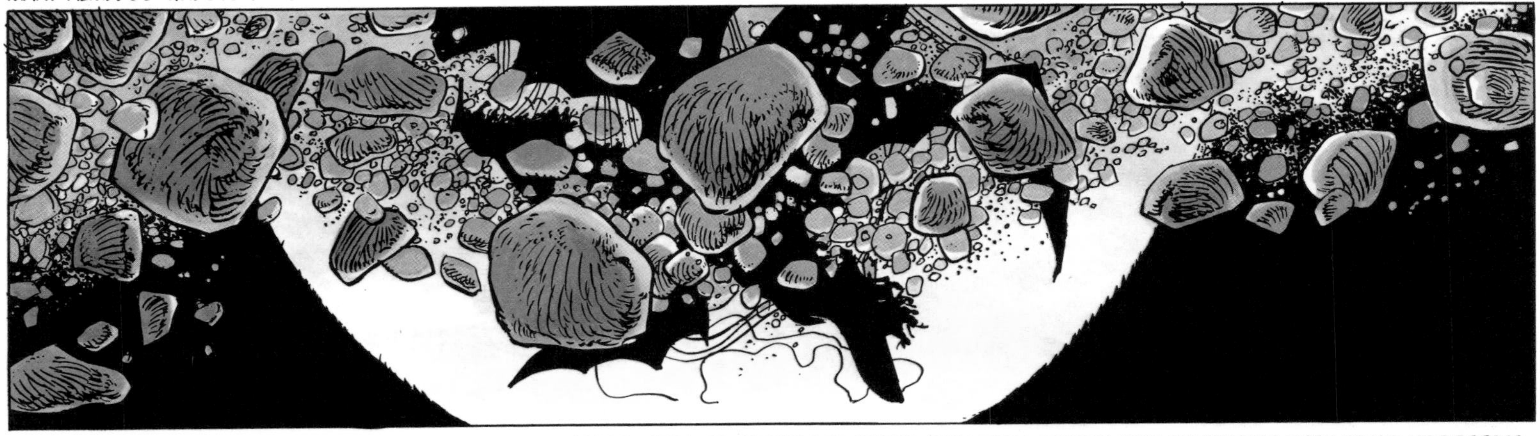

...YET THE OTHERS, THOSE THAT ALWAYS CAME FROM ELSEWHERE, WERE NEVERTHELESS THERE, THEY TOO LOOKING FOR SOMETHING THEY COULD NOT DEFINE.

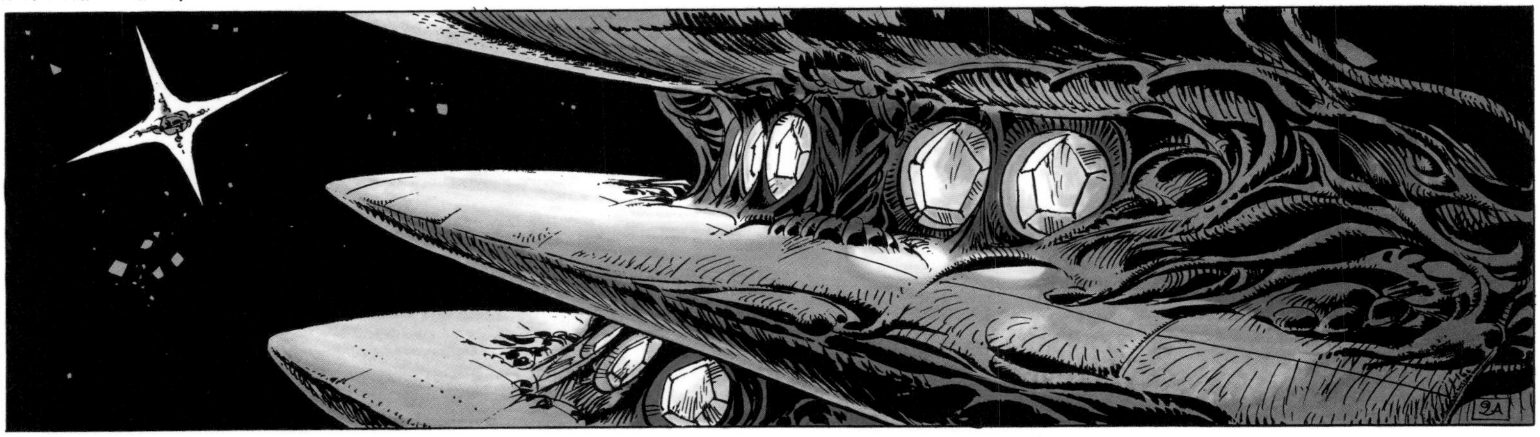

WHAT WERE THE FIRST ENCOUNTERS LIKE? UNFORGIVABLE WARS OR SPONTANEOUS FRATERNISATION?...

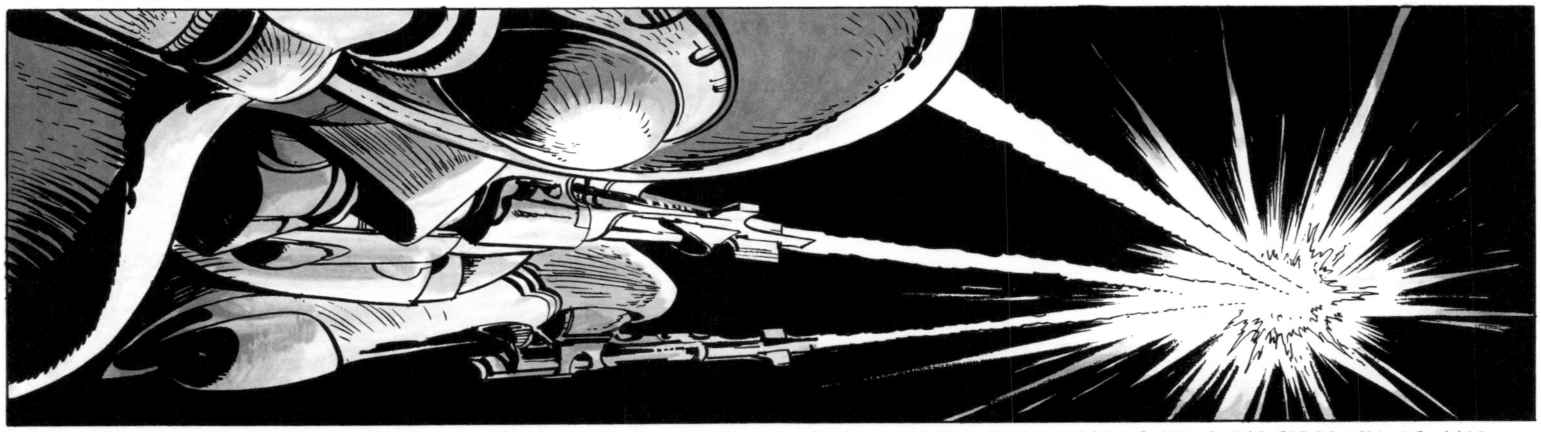

NO ONE REMEMBERS. THE ONLY CERTAINTY IS THAT ONE DAY, AT THE CENTRE OF THE MOST TRAVELLED PATHS OF SPACE, THE FIRST CELL OF WHAT WOULD BECOME **POINT CENTRAL** WAS ERECTED.

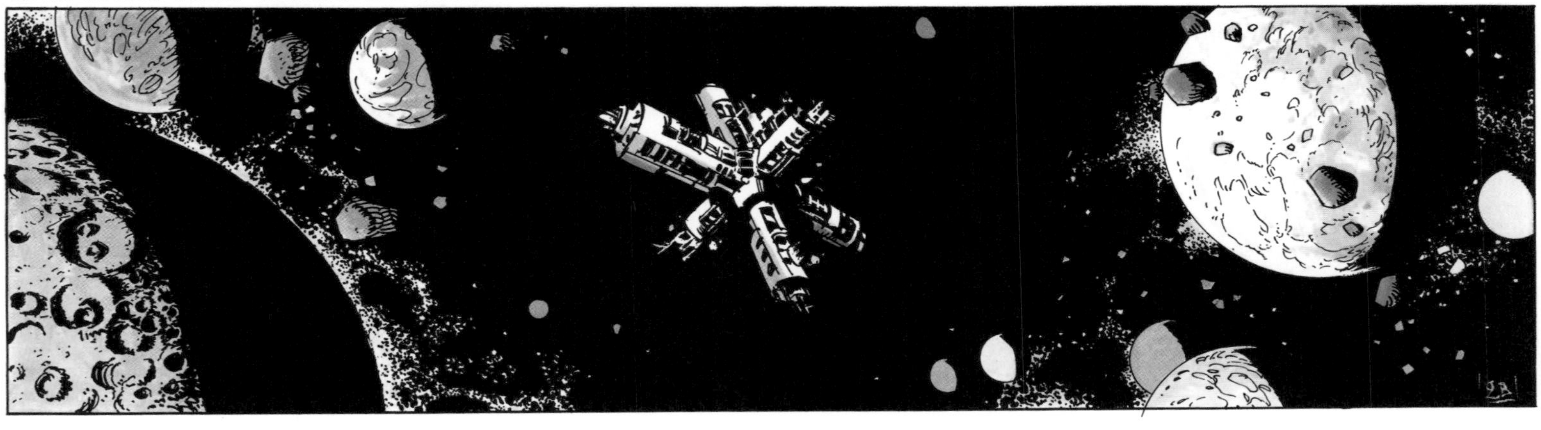

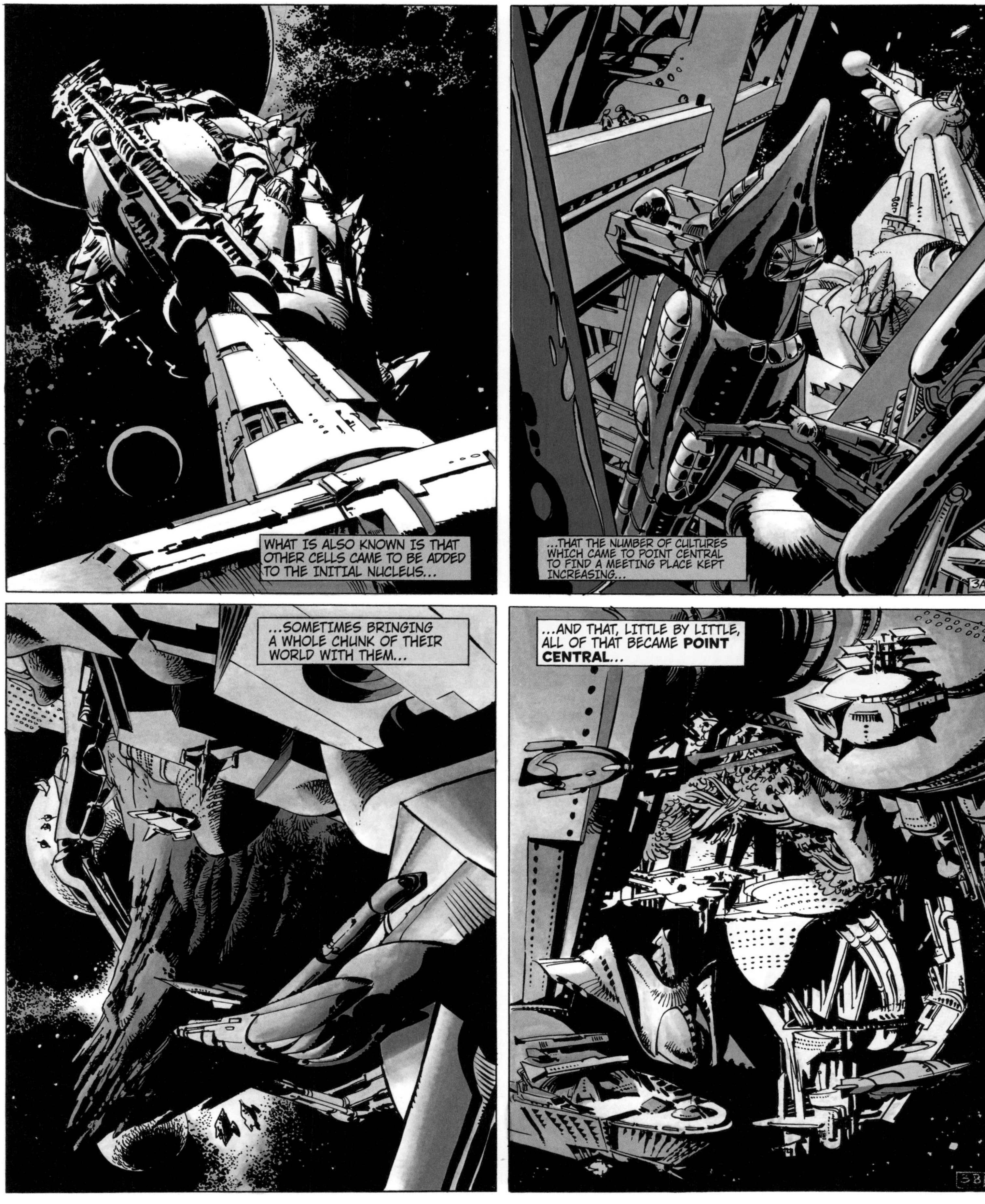
WHAT IS ALSO KNOWN IS THAT OTHER CELLS CAME TO BE ADDED TO THE INITIAL NUCLEUS...
...THAT THE NUMBER OF CULTURES WHICH CAME TO POINT CENTRAL TO FIND A MEETING PLACE KEPT INCREASING...
3A
...SOMETIMES BRINGING A WHOLE CHUNK OF THEIR WORLD WITH THEM...
...AND THAT, LITTLE BY LITTLE, ALL OF THAT BECAME POINT CENTRAL...
3B

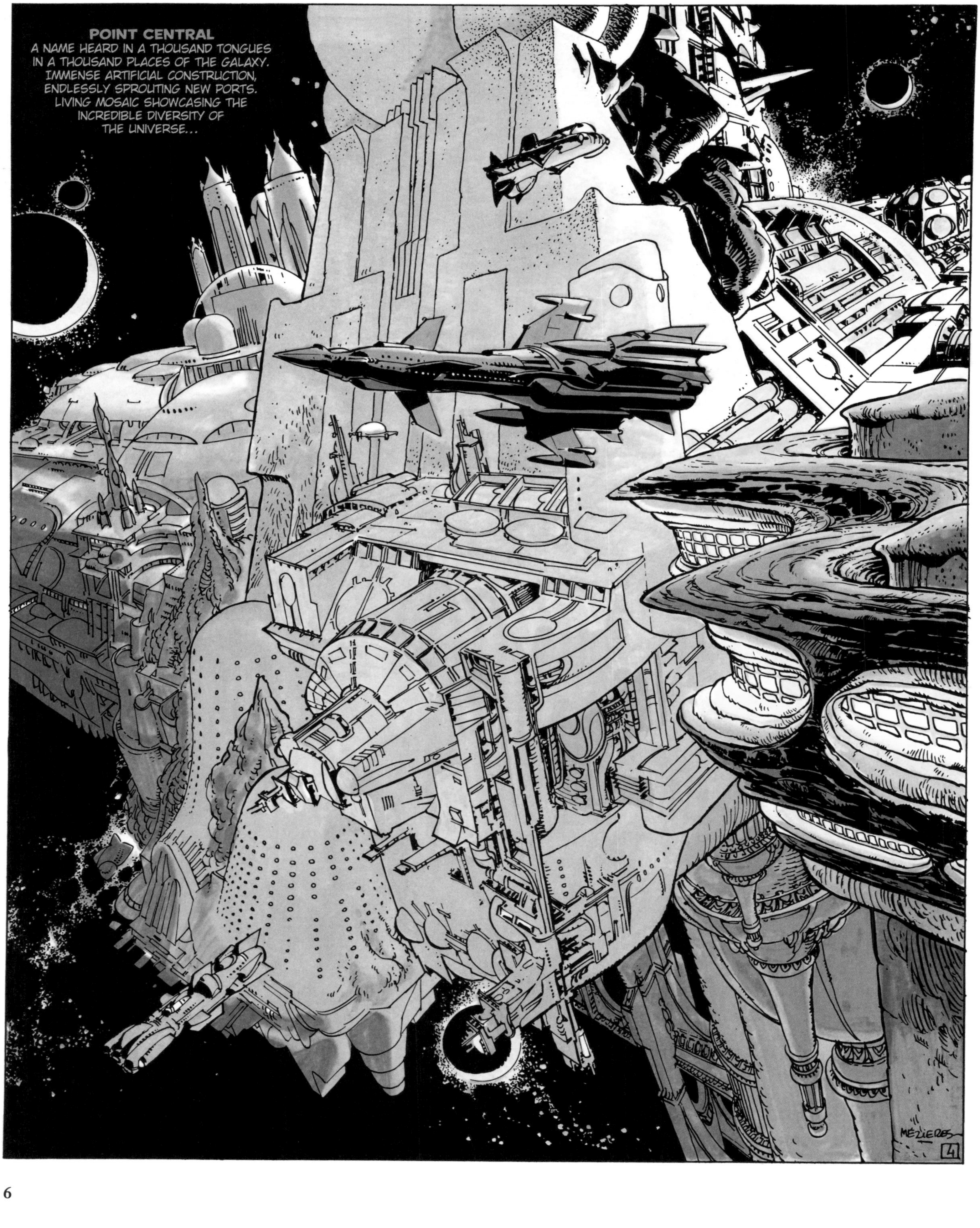
POINT CENTRAL
A NAME HEARD IN A THOUSAND TONGUES
IN A THOUSAND PLACES OF THE GALAXY.
IMMENSE ARTIFICIAL CONSTRUCTION,
ENDLESSLY SPROUTING NEW PORTS.
LIVING MOSAIC SHOWCASING THE
INCREDIBLE DIVERSITY OF
THE UNIVERSE...
MÉZIÈRES
4

INSIDE, AMONG A JUMBLE OF RECONSTITUTED ATMOSPHERES AND ARTIFICIAL GRAVITIES, SEPARATED BY IMPREGNABLE WALLS, SPECIES WITH NOTHING IN COMMON COEXIST: THE ROORS, NATURAL MATHEMATICIANS WHOSE BODIES EXUDE POISONS DEADLY TO ANY OTHER ORGANISM...

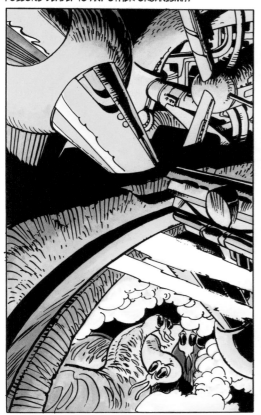

...THE MARMAKAS, FEARED FOR THEIR DREADFUL RADIOACTIVITY BUT FAMED FOR THEIR TALENT AS PSYCHOLOGISTS...

...THE PULPISSIMS, WHOSE FINE PRODUCTS ARE ALL THE RAGE IN MANY A CELL...

...AND THE TAGLIANS, WHO ARE CONSULTED ON ALL THE THEOLOGICAL DISPUTES OF THE UNIVERSE.

THERE IS NO CENTRAL AUTHORITY ON POINT CENTRAL. AMBASSADORS FROM ALL FOUR CORNERS OF SPACE TAKE TURNS PRESIDING OVER THE COUNCIL FROM THE GIGANTIC HALL OF SCREENS. AND IT'S THERE, IN THE LOW-LIT SILENCE, THAT EVERY CONFLICT TEARING AT THE GALAXY'S HISTORICAL FRAME EVENTUALLY EMERGES.

7

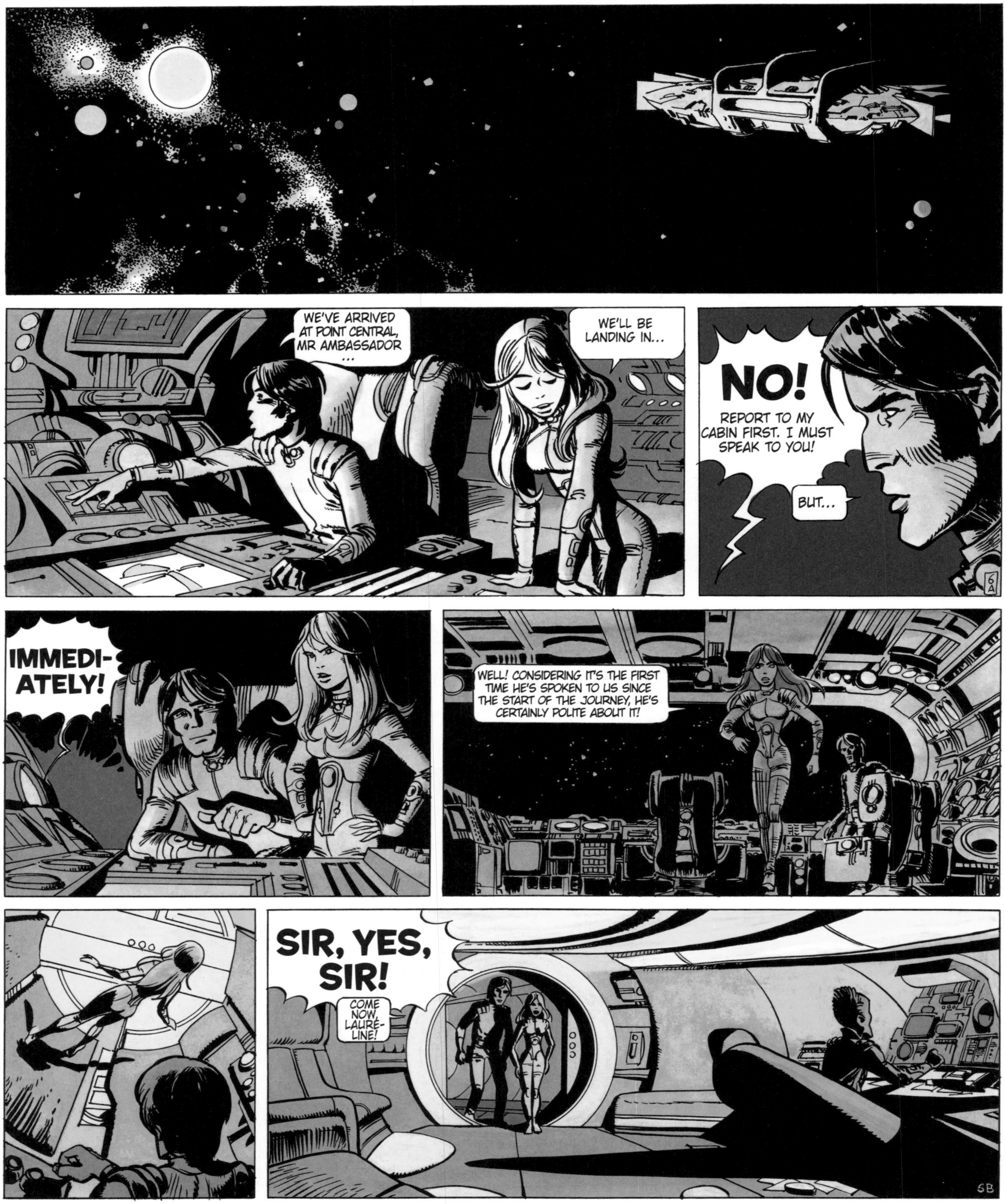
WE'VE ARRIVED AT POINT CENTRAL, MR AMBASSADOR ...
WE'LL BE LANDING IN...
NO!
REPORT TO MY CABIN FIRST. I MUST SPEAK TO YOU!
BUT...
IMMEDI-ATELY!
WELL! CONSIDERING IT'S THE FIRST TIME HE'S SPOKEN TO US SINCE THE START OF THE JOURNEY, HE'S CERTAINLY POLITE ABOUT IT!
SIR, YES, SIR!
COME NOW, LAURÉ-LINE!

DON'T BOTHER, VALERIAN! I'M AWARE OF YOUR REPUTATION, AND IF I CHOSE YOU TWO IT'S NOT OUT OF PERSONAL PREFERENCE...

...IT'S BECAUSE I NEED AGENTS FAMILIAR WITH ALIEN PSYCHES.

AS YOU'RE AWARE, FOR THE FIRST TIME IT'S EARTH'S TURN TO PRESIDE OVER POINT CENTRAL'S COUNCIL. NOW I'M READY TO STRIKE A DECISIVE BLOW! YOU KNOW AS WELL AS I DO HOW INCOHERENT AND CHAOTIC THE ADMINISTRATION OF SPACE IS. WELL, I INTEND TO BRING SOME ORDER TO IT...

WHAT DO YOU MEAN? NO ONE TOLD US ABOUT THIS BEFORE WE LEFT!

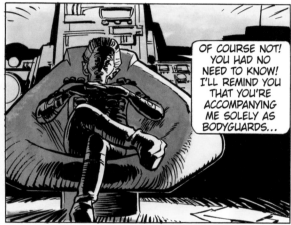

OF COURSE NOT! YOU HAD NO NEED TO KNOW! I'LL REMIND YOU THAT YOU'RE ACCOMPANYING ME SOLELY AS BODYGUARDS...

IN THAT CASE, IF I'M ONLY HERE TO SHIELD YOU WITH MY BODY, I'LL GO AND GRAB MY BLASTER!... NO NEED FOR A SPEECH...

STAY HERE!... AND LISTEN TO ME!

ER... I'M LISTENING, SIR...

HMM!... YES... IT'S IMPOSSIBLE TO TRADE IN PEACE OR TO ORGANISE METHODICAL EXPLORATION MISSIONS. SPACE ROUTES AREN'T SAFE, AND ALL SORTS OF CRANKS HAVE FAILED TO UNDERSTAND THAT THE EMERGENCE OF EARTH MARKED THE DAWN OF A NEW ERA...

OUR TECHNICAL POTENTIAL GIVES US ABSOLUTE SUPREMACY. I AM THEREFORE GOING TO PROPOSE THE CREATION OF A SORT OF FEDERATION, OF WHICH WE WOULD BE THE CORNERSTONE...

...AND THE POLICE!!

SPEAK RATHER OF A CIVILISING MISSION, MY GOOD FELLOW. TRUST ME, THERE ARE NUMEROUS PEOPLE WHO, EVEN UNCONSCIOUSLY, LONG FOR OUR ACTION...

UNCONSCIOUSLY? PFFF...

IT WILL BE A HARD SALE, EVEN THOUGH WE ALREADY HAVE A FEW ALLIES IN PLACE AND ... ER ... SOME EXTERNAL ASSETS!

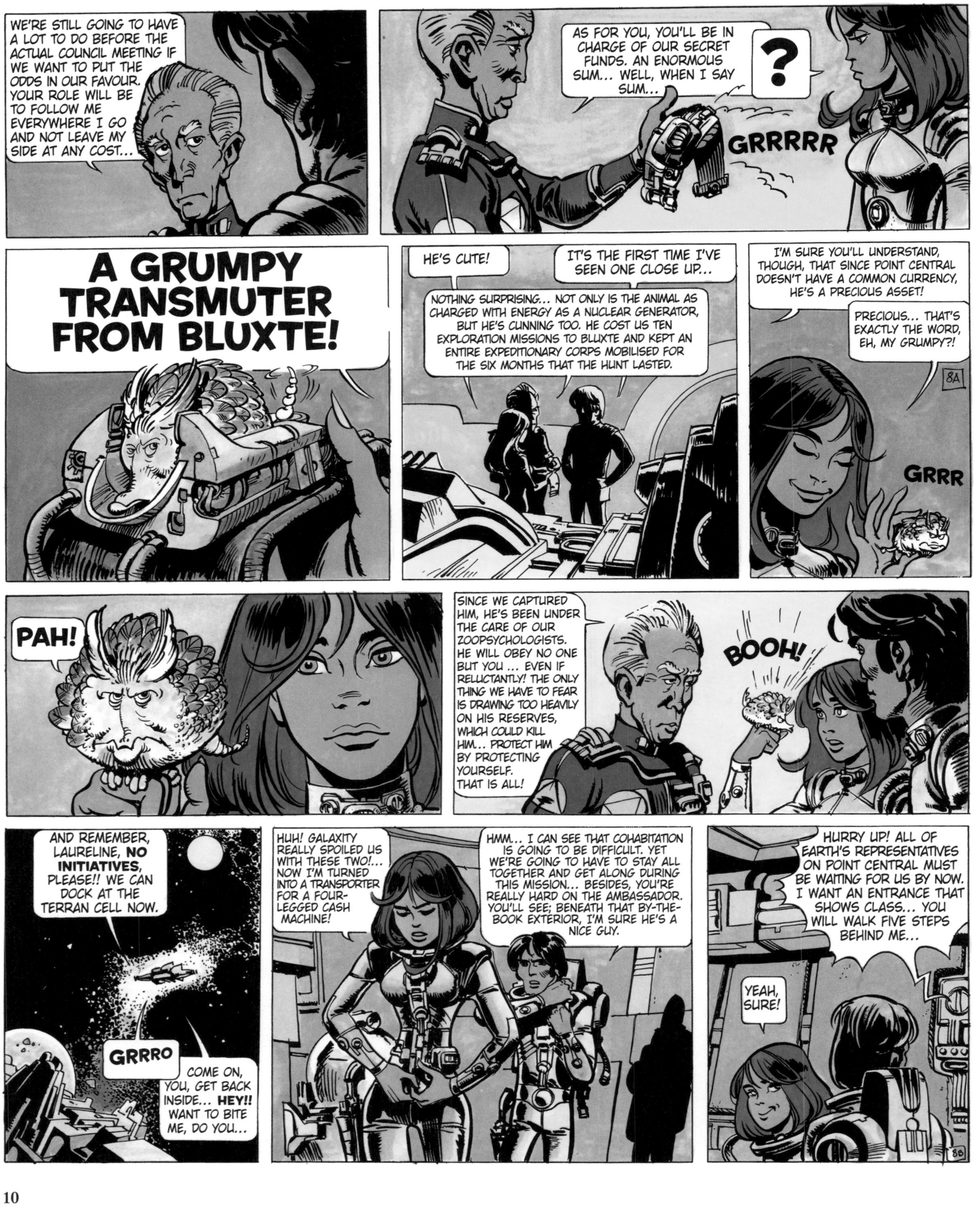

WE'RE STILL GOING TO HAVE A LOT TO DO BEFORE THE ACTUAL COUNCIL MEETING IF WE WANT TO PUT THE ODDS IN OUR FAVOUR. YOUR ROLE WILL BE TO FOLLOW ME EVERYWHERE I GO AND NOT LEAVE MY SIDE AT ANY COST...
AS FOR YOU, YOU'LL BE IN CHARGE OF OUR SECRET FUNDS. AN ENORMOUS SUM... WELL, WHEN I SAY SUM...
?
GRRRRR
A GRUMPY TRANSMUTER FROM BLUXTE!
HE'S CUTE!
IT'S THE FIRST TIME I'VE SEEN ONE CLOSE UP...
NOTHING SURPRISING... NOT ONLY IS THE ANIMAL AS CHARGED WITH ENERGY AS A NUCLEAR GENERATOR, BUT HE'S CUNNING TOO. HE COST US TEN EXPLORATION MISSIONS TO BLUXTE AND KEPT AN ENTIRE EXPEDITIONARY CORPS MOBILISED FOR THE SIX MONTHS THAT THE HUNT LASTED.
I'M SURE YOU'LL UNDERSTAND, THOUGH, THAT SINCE POINT CENTRAL DOESN'T HAVE A COMMON CURRENCY, HE'S A PRECIOUS ASSET!
PRECIOUS... THAT'S EXACTLY THE WORD, EH, MY GRUMPY?!
8A
GRRR
PAH!
SINCE WE CAPTURED HIM, HE'S BEEN UNDER THE CARE OF OUR ZOOPSYCHOLOGISTS. HE WILL OBEY NO ONE BUT YOU ... EVEN IF RELUCTANTLY! THE ONLY THING WE HAVE TO FEAR IS DRAWING TOO HEAVILY ON HIS RESERVES, WHICH COULD KILL HIM... PROTECT HIM BY PROTECTING YOURSELF. THAT IS ALL!
BOOH!
AND REMEMBER, LAURELINE, NO INITIATIVES, PLEASE!! WE CAN DOCK AT THE TERRAN CELL NOW.
GRRRO
COME ON, YOU, GET BACK INSIDE... HEY!! WANT TO BITE ME, DO YOU...
HUH! GALAXITY REALLY SPOILED US WITH THESE TWO!... NOW I'M TURNED INTO A TRANSPORTER FOR A FOUR-LEGGED CASH MACHINE!
HMM... I CAN SEE THAT COHABITATION IS GOING TO BE DIFFICULT. YET WE'RE GOING TO HAVE TO STAY ALL TOGETHER AND GET ALONG DURING THIS MISSION... BESIDES, YOU'RE REALLY HARD ON THE AMBASSADOR. YOU'LL SEE; BENEATH THAT BY-THE-BOOK EXTERIOR, I'M SURE HE'S A NICE GUY.
HURRY UP! ALL OF EARTH'S REPRESENTATIVES ON POINT CENTRAL MUST BE WAITING FOR US BY NOW. I WANT AN ENTRANCE THAT SHOWS CLASS... YOU WILL WALK FIVE STEPS BEHIND ME...
YEAH, SURE!
8B

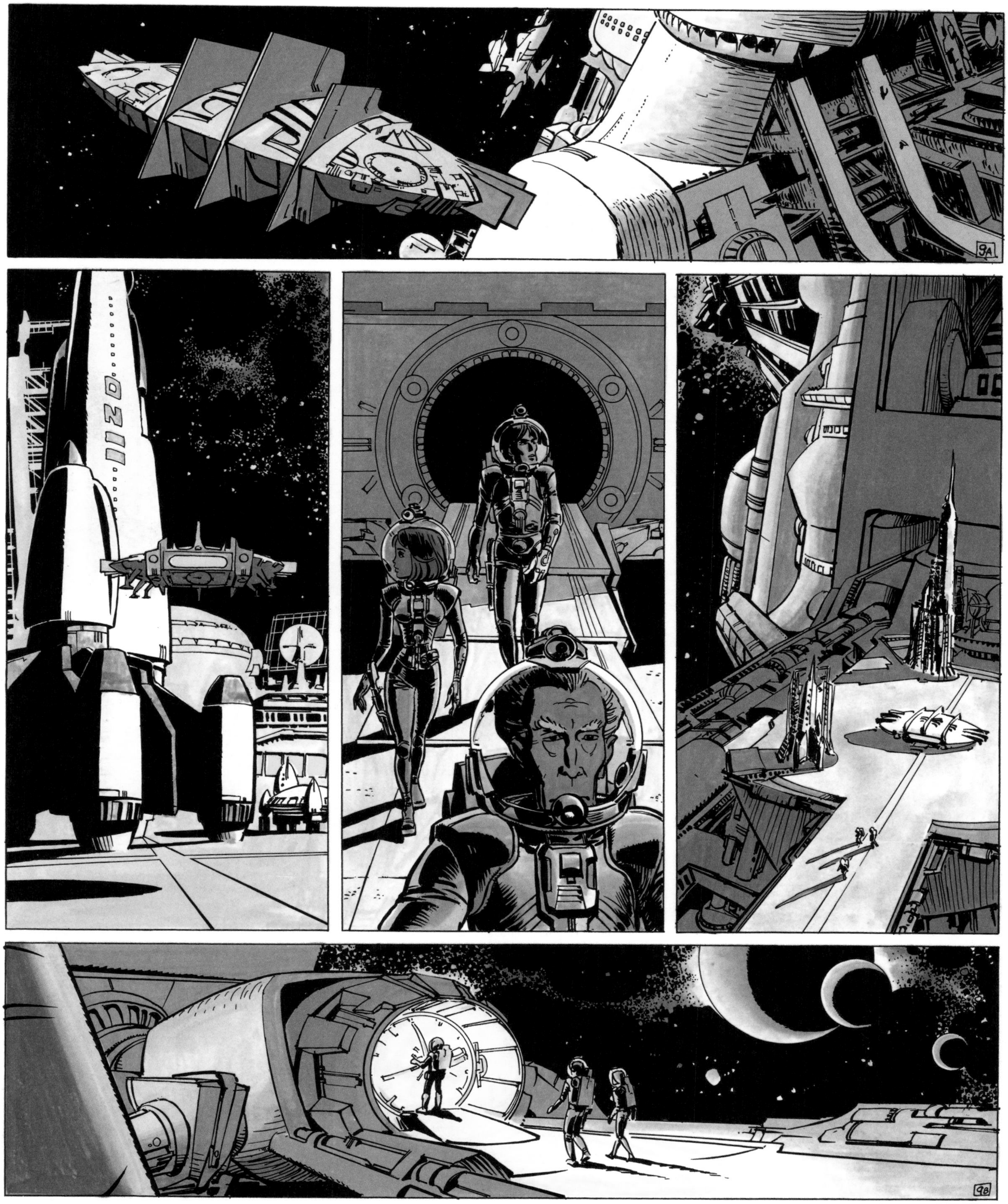
9A
9B

MY FELLOW
...

SSSSS

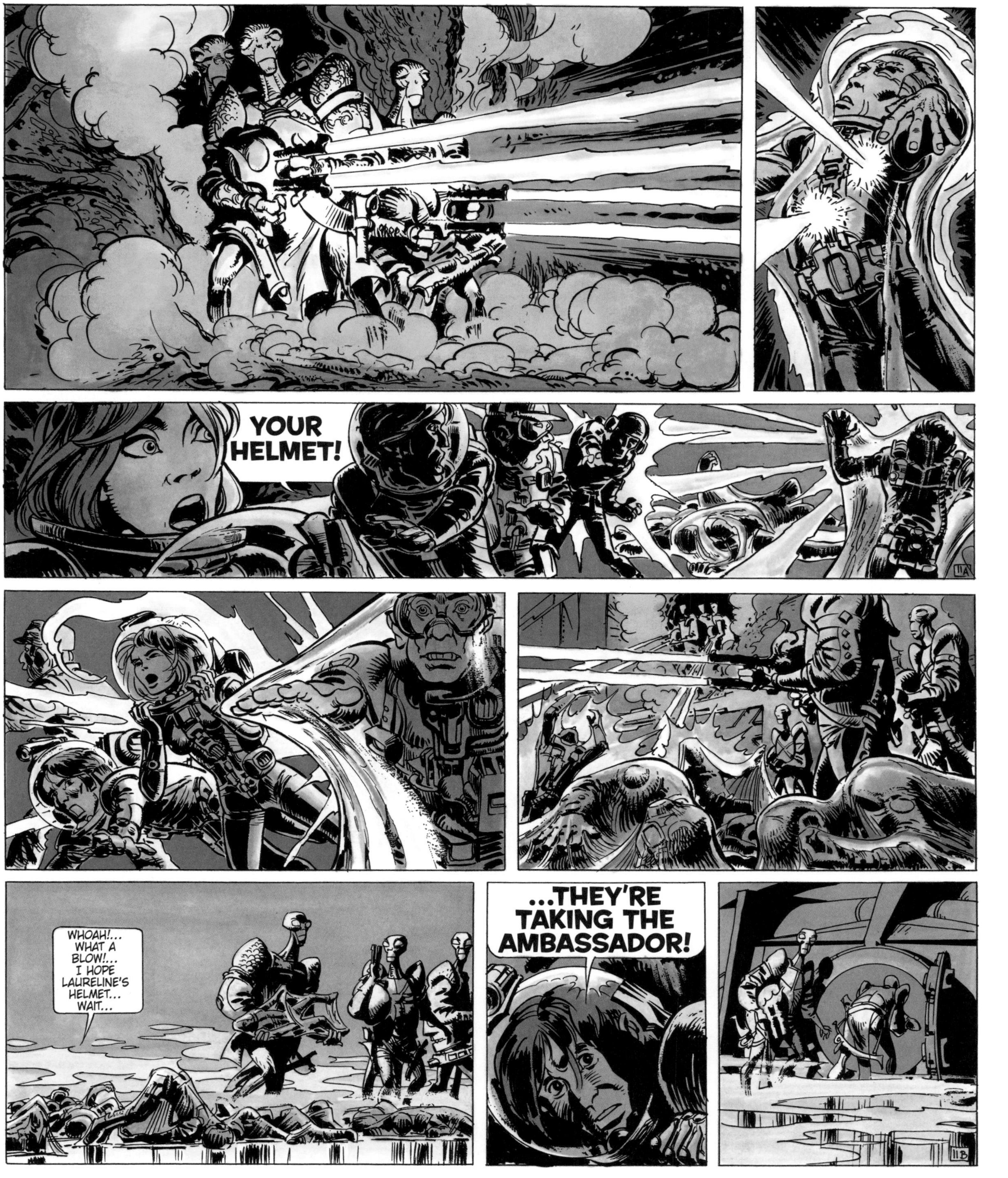
YOUR HELMET!
WHOAH!... WHAT A BLOW!... I HOPE LAURELINE'S HELMET... WAIT...
...THEY'RE TAKING THE AMBASSADOR!

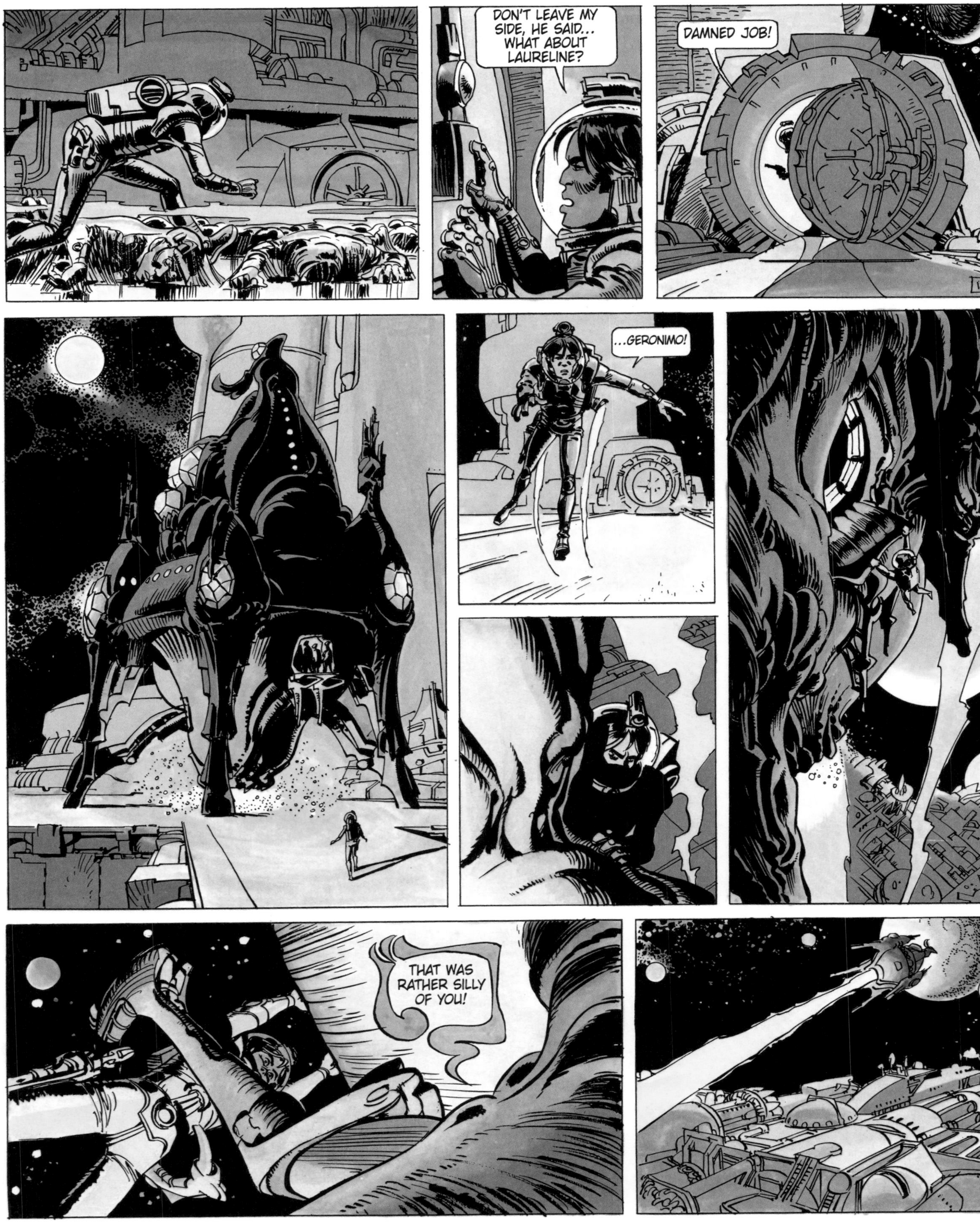
DON'T LEAVE MY SIDE, HE SAID... WHAT ABOUT LAURELINE?
DAMNED JOB!
12A
...GERONIMO!
THAT WAS RATHER SILLY OF YOU!
12C

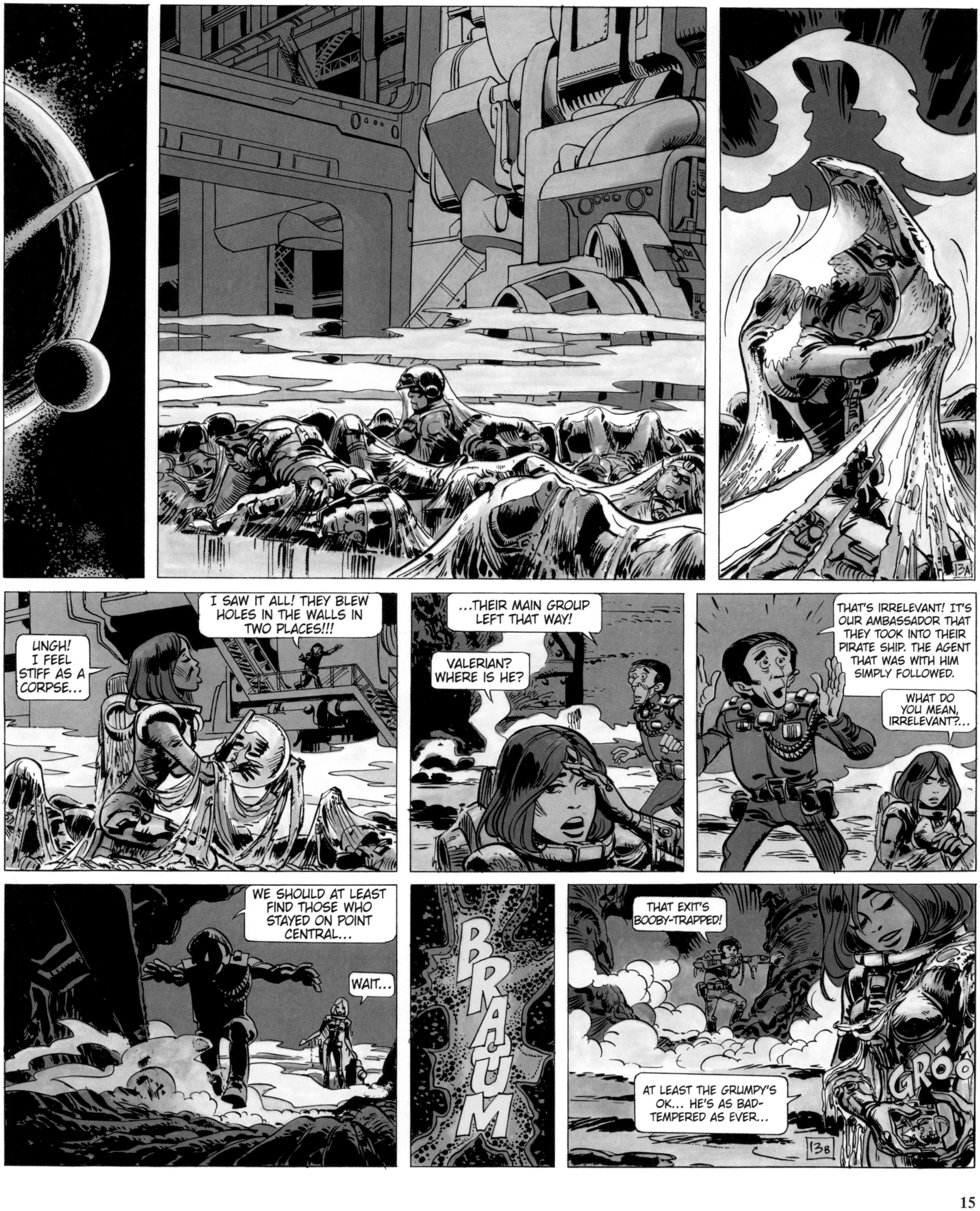

13A
UNGH! I FEEL STIFF AS A CORPSE...
I SAW IT ALL! THEY BLEW HOLES IN THE WALLS IN TWO PLACES!!!
...THEIR MAIN GROUP LEFT THAT WAY!
VALERIAN? WHERE IS HE?
THAT'S IRRELEVANT! IT'S OUR AMBASSADOR THAT THEY TOOK INTO THEIR PIRATE SHIP. THE AGENT THAT WAS WITH HIM SIMPLY FOLLOWED.
WHAT DO YOU MEAN, IRRELEVANT?...
WE SHOULD AT LEAST FIND THOSE WHO STAYED ON POINT CENTRAL...
WAIT...
BRAAUM
THAT EXIT'S BOOBY-TRAPPED!
AT LEAST THE GRUMPY'S OK... HE'S AS BAD-TEMPERED AS EVER...
GROO
13B

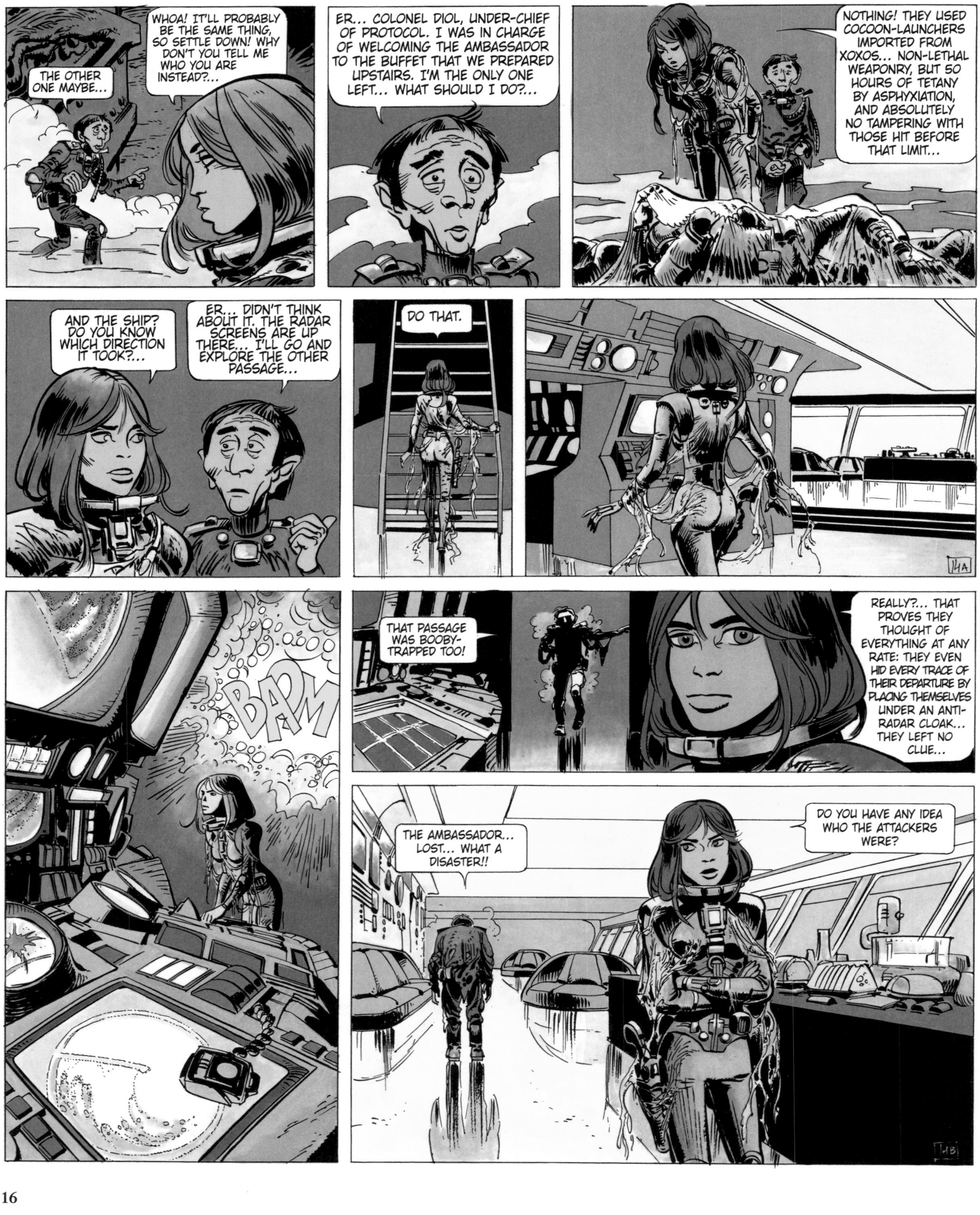
WHOA! IT'LL PROBABLY BE THE SAME THING, SO SETTLE DOWN! WHY DON'T YOU TELL ME WHO YOU ARE INSTEAD?...
THE OTHER ONE MAYBE...
ER... COLONEL DIOL, UNDER-CHIEF OF PROTOCOL. I WAS IN CHARGE OF WELCOMING THE AMBASSADOR TO THE BUFFET THAT WE PREPARED UPSTAIRS. I'M THE ONLY ONE LEFT... WHAT SHOULD I DO?...
NOTHING! THEY USED COCOON-LAUNCHERS IMPORTED FROM XOXOS... NON-LETHAL WEAPONRY, BUT 50 HOURS OF TETANY BY ASPHYXIATION, AND ABSOLUTELY NO TAMPERING WITH THOSE HIT BEFORE THAT LIMIT...
AND THE SHIP? DO YOU KNOW WHICH DIRECTION IT TOOK?...
ER... DIDN'T THINK ABOUT IT. THE RADAR SCREENS ARE UP THERE... I'LL GO AND EXPLORE THE OTHER PASSAGE...
DO THAT.
14A
BAM
THAT PASSAGE WAS BOOBY-TRAPPED TOO!
REALLY?... THAT PROVES THEY THOUGHT OF EVERYTHING AT ANY RATE: THEY EVEN HID EVERY TRACE OF THEIR DEPARTURE BY PLACING THEMSELVES UNDER AN ANTI-RADAR CLOAK... THEY LEFT NO CLUE...
THE AMBASSADOR... LOST... WHAT A DISASTER!!
DO YOU HAVE ANY IDEA WHO THE ATTACKERS WERE?
14B

NONE! THERE ARE THOUSAND OF SPECIES ON POINT CENTRAL, AND MY JOB'S ORGANISING RECEPTIONS... MY BEAUTIFUL RECEPTION!... EVERYTHING WAS READY FOR THE AMBASSADOR!!!

WE HAVE TO TELL EARTH! CALL IN THE MILITARY!!!... BECAUSE ... POINT CENTRAL...

WHAT DO YOU ... CRUNCH ... MEAN?...

BAH! IT'S COMPLETE ANARCHY! NO ONE KNOWS ANYTHING ABOUT ANYTHING! EVERYWHERE IT'S A FREE-FOR-ALL... ONLY THE COUNCIL HAS A MEASURE OF POWER, BUT SINCE THERE WON'T BE A COUNCIL MEETING UNLESS WE FIND THE AMBASSADOR...

YES... I WONDER ... MUNCH ... WHAT...

BUZZZ

BUZZZ

IT'S THEM! THEY'RE BACK! LET'S HIDE!...

YEAH, RIGHT! AND THEY'D POLITELY KNOCK ON THE DOOR OF THE MAIN HATCH?... BESIDES, LOOK...

WE'RE EXPECTED...

...THESE ONES ARE COMPLETELY DIFFERENT... WHY DON'T YOU SHOW ME HOW TO OPEN THE HATCH?...

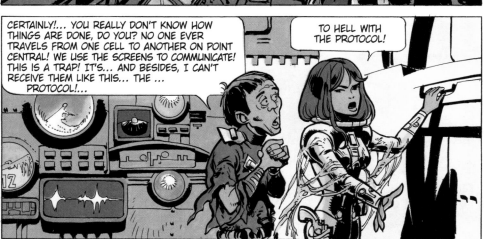

CERTAINLY!... YOU REALLY DON'T KNOW HOW THINGS ARE DONE, DO YOU? NO ONE EVER TRAVELS FROM ONE CELL TO ANOTHER ON POINT CENTRAL! WE USE THE SCREENS TO COMMUNICATE! THIS IS A TRAP! IT'S... AND BESIDES, I CAN'T RECEIVE THEM LIKE THIS... THE ... PROTOCOL!...

TO HELL WITH THE PROTOCOL!

DO YOU REPRESENT EARTH?...

ER, YES...

NO, NO...

IS IT YES OR NO?... BECAUSE WE'VE RECEIVED PROMISES...

YOU DON'T KNOW WHO WE ARE?... THE SHINGOUZ...

WE HAD A MEETING WITH THE AMBASSADOR TO SELL HIM SOME BITS OF INFORMATION... IS HE AROUND?...

INTERESTING... YOU DON'T SOUND THAT WELL INFORMED TO ME...

THAT DEPENDS, THAT DEPENDS... WE HAVE A CERTAIN REPUTATION ON POINT CENTRAL... WE HEAR AND SEE MANY THINGS...

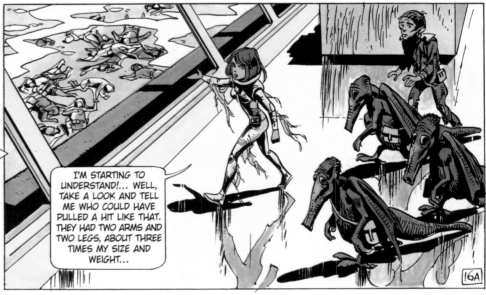

I'M STARTING TO UNDERSTAND!... WELL, TAKE A LOOK AND TELL ME WHO COULD HAVE PULLED A HIT LIKE THAT. THEY HAD TWO ARMS AND TWO LEGS, ABOUT THREE TIMES MY SIZE AND WEIGHT...

16A

BY THE TEN PURPLE MOONS! XOXOS COCOONS!! NEVER SEEN ANYTHING LIKE IT ON POINT CENTRAL!

AND THE ATTACKERS?...

BIG, TWO ARMS, TWO LEGS... YOU DON'T REALISE — THAT COULD BE ANYBODY...

MERCENARIES, PROBABLY, TO BE USING SUCH METHODS! NONE OF THE MAJOR SPECIES WOULD WANT TO BE MIXED UP IN THIS...

FOR 1,000 EBEBE PEARLS LIKE THIS ONE...

A THOUSAND EBEBE PEARLS?! IS THAT ALL?!

WHEN YOU'RE LUCKY ENOUGH TO OWN A TRANSMUTER, YOU SHOULDN'T BE STINGY... BESIDES, OUR INFORMATION IS WELL WORTH IT!

GRÔ'O

IT'S NOT THE ONE WE CAME HERE TO SELL YOU, BUT IT'S STILL A GOOD PIECE OF INFORMATION FOR YOU, SINCE YOUR AMBASSADOR OBVIOUSLY DIDN'T SHARE ALL HIS BUSINESS WITH YOU...

...THIS HIT IS TOO RECENT FOR US TO KNOW WHO DID IT. BUT EARTH HAS SOME SECRET ALLIES, MERCENARIES THEMSELVES. SUCH PEOPLE KNOW EACH OTHER... YOU KNOW HOW IT IS: YOU WORK FOR ONE SIDE, THEN FOR ANOTHER...

16B

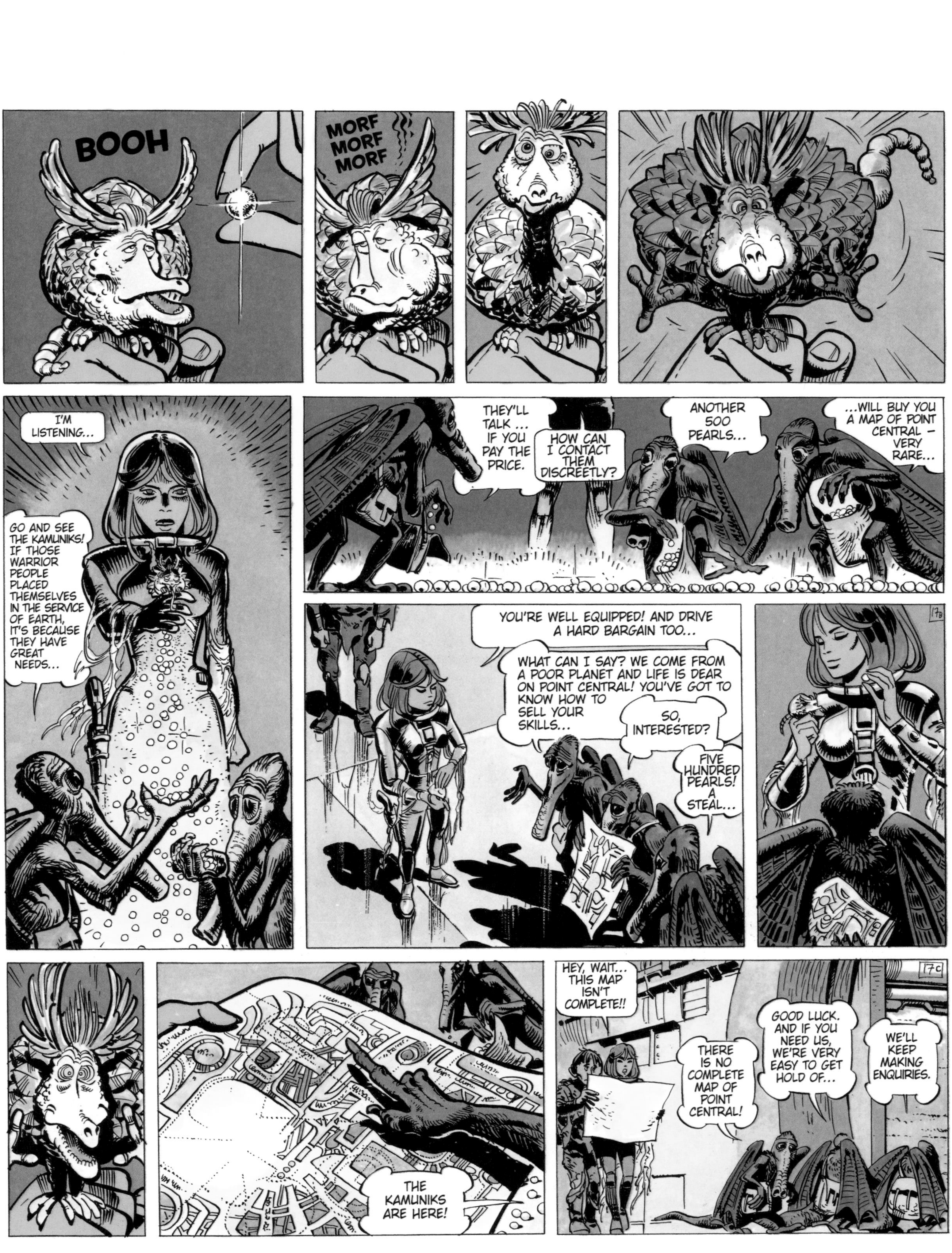
BOOH
MORF MORF MORF
I'M LISTENING...
GO AND SEE THE KAMUNIKS! IF THOSE WARRIOR PEOPLE PLACED THEMSELVES IN THE SERVICE OF EARTH, IT'S BECAUSE THEY HAVE GREAT NEEDS...
HOW CAN I CONTACT THEM DISCREETLY?
THEY'LL TALK ... IF YOU PAY THE PRICE.
ANOTHER 500 PEARLS...
...WILL BUY YOU A MAP OF POINT CENTRAL – VERY RARE...
YOU'RE WELL EQUIPPED! AND DRIVE A HARD BARGAIN TOO...
WHAT CAN I SAY? WE COME FROM A POOR PLANET AND LIFE IS DEAR ON POINT CENTRAL! YOU'VE GOT TO KNOW HOW TO SELL YOUR SKILLS...
SO, INTERESTED?
FIVE HUNDRED PEARLS! A STEAL...
17B
THE KAMUNIKS ARE HERE!
17C
HEY, WAIT... THIS MAP ISN'T COMPLETE!!
THERE IS NO COMPLETE MAP OF POINT CENTRAL!
GOOD LUCK. AND IF YOU NEED US, WE'RE VERY EASY TO GET HOLD OF...
WE'LL KEEP MAKING ENQUIRIES.

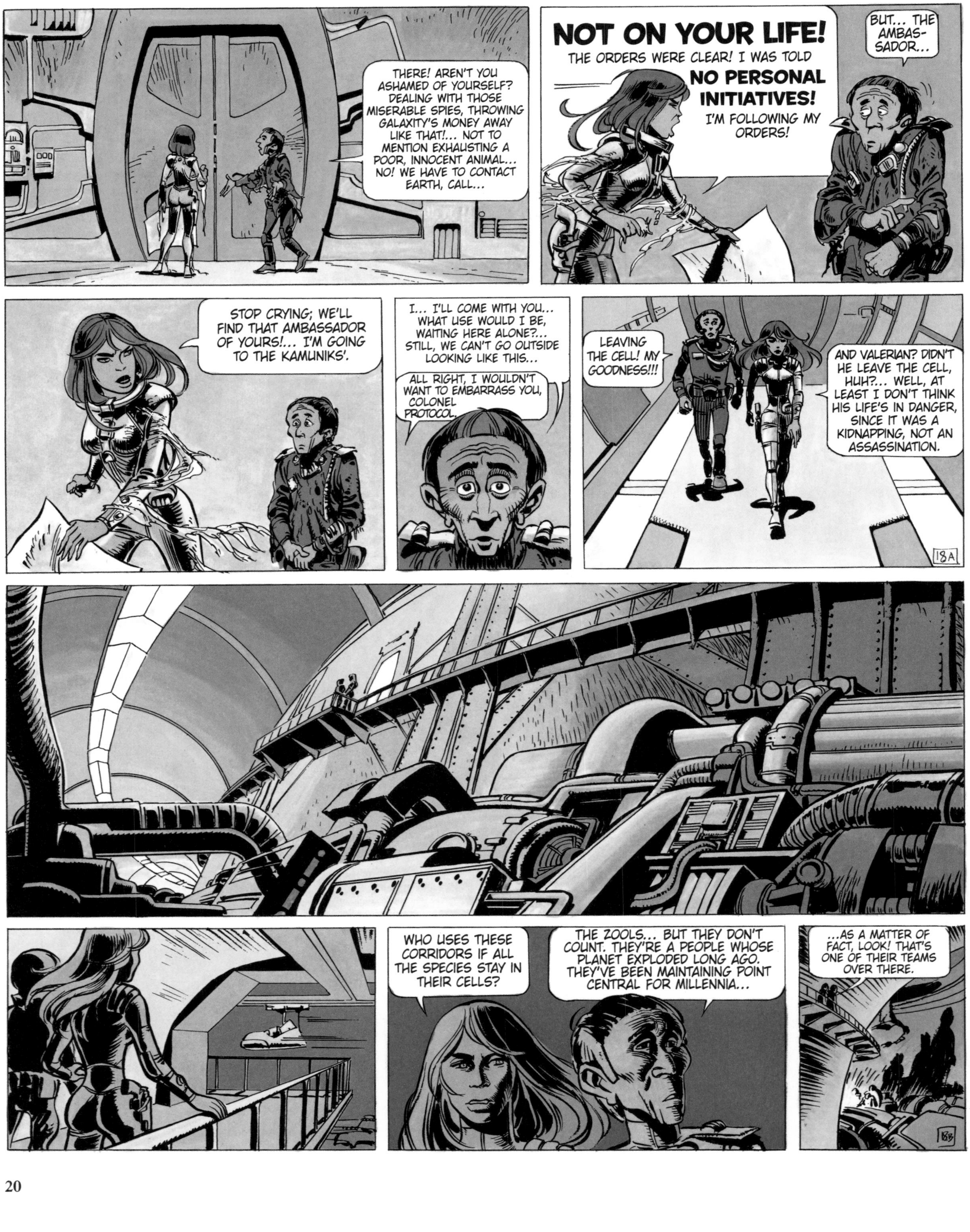
THERE! AREN'T YOU ASHAMED OF YOURSELF? DEALING WITH THOSE MISERABLE SPIES, THROWING GALAXITY'S MONEY AWAY LIKE THAT!... NOT TO MENTION EXHAUSTING A POOR, INNOCENT ANIMAL... NO! WE HAVE TO CONTACT EARTH, CALL...
NOT ON YOUR LIFE! THE ORDERS WERE CLEAR! I WAS TOLD NO PERSONAL INITIATIVES! I'M FOLLOWING MY ORDERS!
BUT... THE AMBAS-SADOR...
STOP CRYING; WE'LL FIND THAT AMBASSADOR OF YOURS!... I'M GOING TO THE KAMUNIKS'.
I... I'LL COME WITH YOU... WHAT USE WOULD I BE, WAITING HERE ALONE?... STILL, WE CAN'T GO OUTSIDE LOOKING LIKE THIS...
ALL RIGHT, I WOULDN'T WANT TO EMBARRASS YOU, COLONEL PROTOCOL.
LEAVING THE CELL! MY GOODNESS!!!
AND VALERIAN? DIDN'T HE LEAVE THE CELL, HUH?... WELL, AT LEAST I DON'T THINK HIS LIFE'S IN DANGER, SINCE IT WAS A KIDNAPPING, NOT AN ASSASSINATION.
18A
WHO USES THESE CORRIDORS IF ALL THE SPECIES STAY IN THEIR CELLS?
THE ZOOLS... BUT THEY DON'T COUNT. THEY'RE A PEOPLE WHOSE PLANET EXPLODED LONG AGO. THEY'VE BEEN MAINTAINING POINT CENTRAL FOR MILLENNIA...
...AS A MATTER OF FACT, LOOK! THAT'S ONE OF THEIR TEAMS OVER THERE.
18B

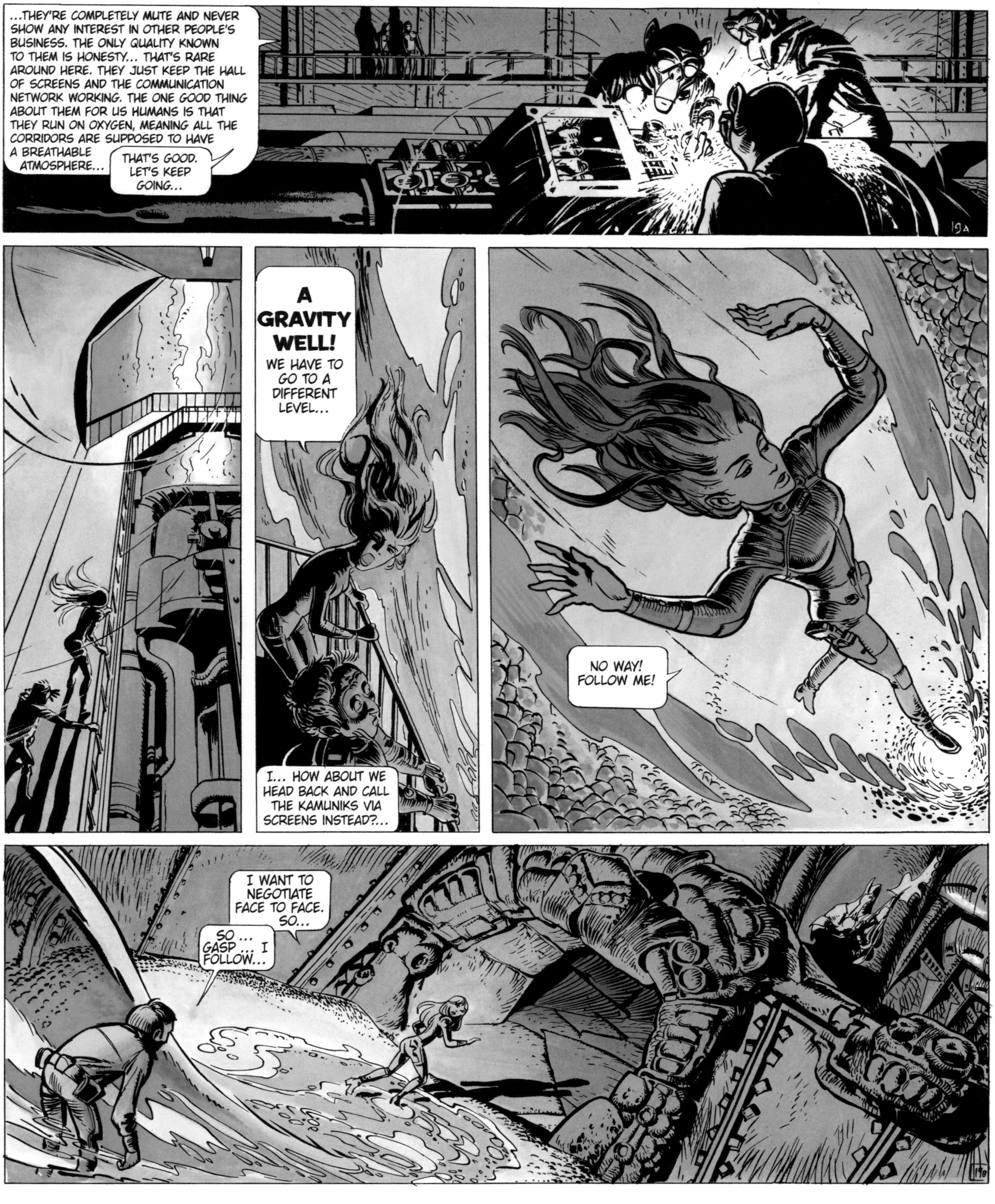
...THEY'RE COMPLETELY MUTE AND NEVER SHOW ANY INTEREST IN OTHER PEOPLE'S BUSINESS. THE ONLY QUALITY KNOWN TO THEM IS HONESTY... THAT'S RARE AROUND HERE. THEY JUST KEEP THE HALL OF SCREENS AND THE COMMUNICATION NETWORK WORKING. THE ONE GOOD THING ABOUT THEM FOR US HUMANS IS THAT THEY RUN ON OXYGEN, MEANING ALL THE CORRIDORS ARE SUPPOSED TO HAVE A BREATHABLE ATMOSPHERE...
THAT'S GOOD. LET'S KEEP GOING...
A GRAVITY WELL! WE HAVE TO GO TO A DIFFERENT LEVEL...
I... HOW ABOUT WE HEAD BACK AND CALL THE KAMUNIKS VIA SCREENS INSTEAD?...
NO WAY! FOLLOW ME!
I WANT TO NEGOTIATE FACE TO FACE. SO...
SO ... GASP ... I FOLLOW...

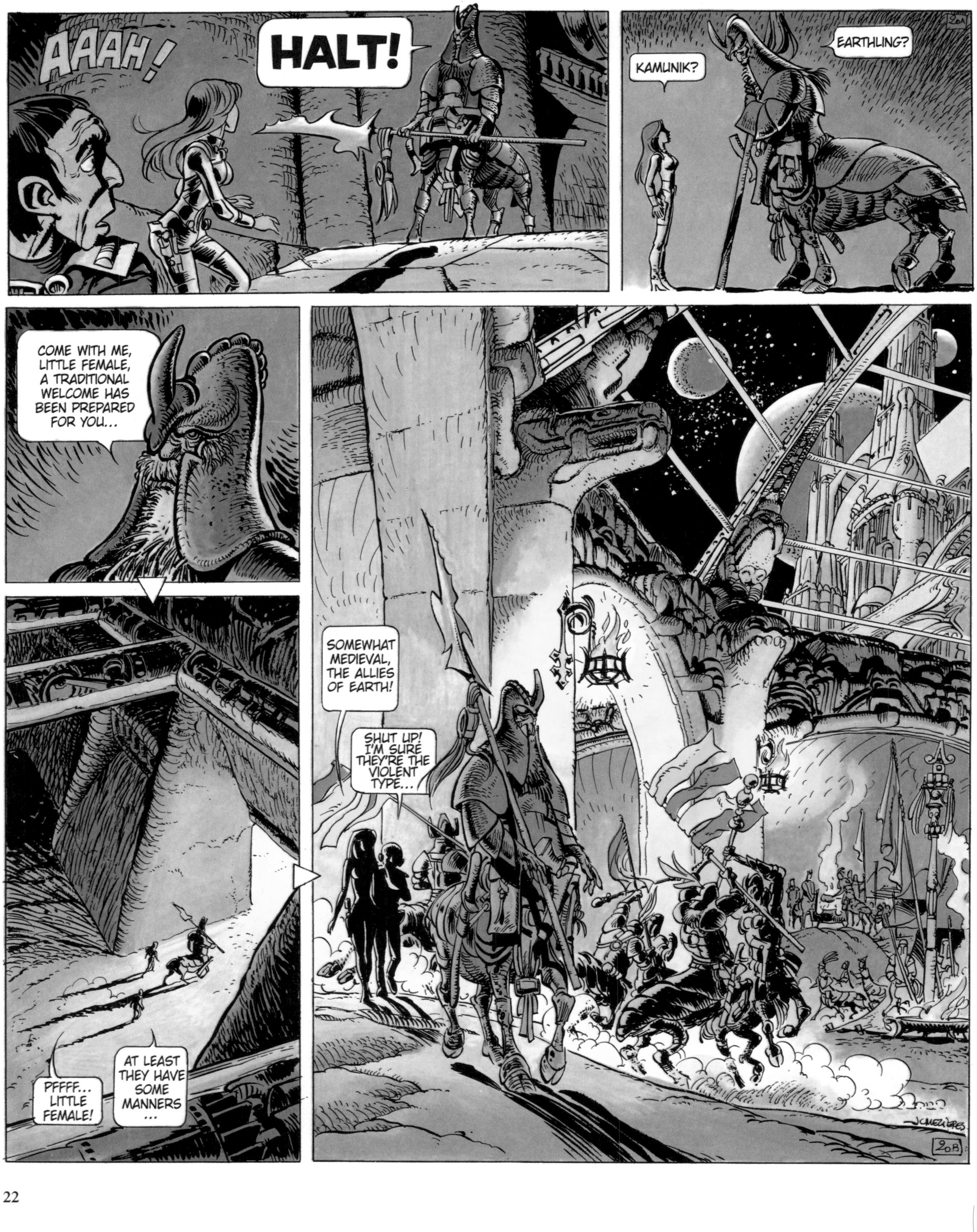

AAAH!
HALT!
KAMUNIK?
EARTHLING?
COME WITH ME, LITTLE FEMALE, A TRADITIONAL WELCOME HAS BEEN PREPARED FOR YOU...
PFFFF... LITTLE FEMALE!
AT LEAST THEY HAVE SOME MANNERS ...
SOMEWHAT MEDIEVAL, THE ALLIES OF EARTH!
SHUT UP! I'M SURE THEY'RE THE VIOLENT TYPE...

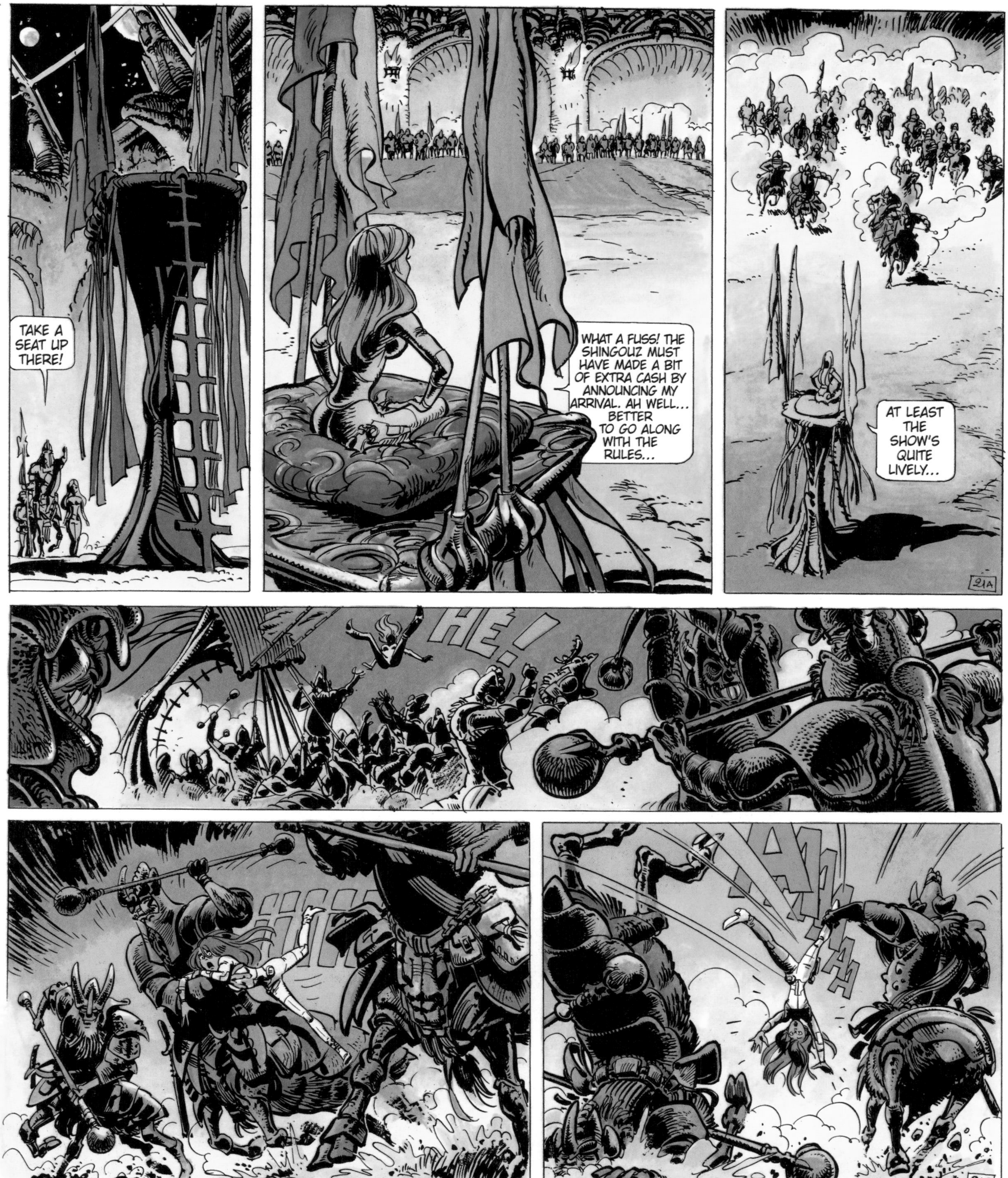
TAKE A SEAT UP THERE!
WHAT A FUSS! THE SHINGOUZ MUST HAVE MADE A BIT OF EXTRA CASH BY ANNOUNCING MY ARRIVAL. AH WELL... BETTER TO GO ALONG WITH THE RULES...
AT LEAST THE SHOW'S QUITE LIVELY...
21A
HE!
21B

COMPLIMENTS, BALDOUR! STILL THE BEST!

SO, WHAT DID YOU COME HERE FOR?

GOOD QUES- TION...

HERE'S THE GUEST!

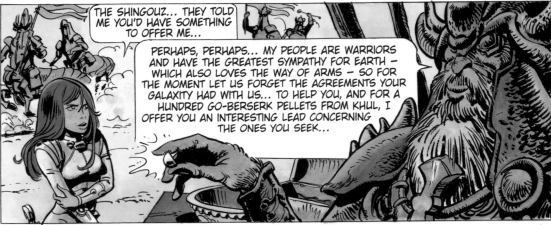

THE SHINGOUZ... THEY TOLD ME YOU'D HAVE SOMETHING TO OFFER ME...

PERHAPS, PERHAPS... MY PEOPLE ARE WARRIORS AND HAVE THE GREATEST SYMPATHY FOR EARTH — WHICH ALSO LOVES THE WAY OF ARMS — SO FOR THE MOMENT LET US FORGET THE AGREEMENTS YOUR GALAXY HAD WITH US... TO HELP YOU, AND FOR A HUNDRED GO-BERSERK PELLETS FROM KHUL, I OFFER YOU AN INTERESTING LEAD CONCERNING THE ONES YOU SEEK...

HMM! THAT CAN BE ARRANGED... COME HERE, GRUMPY, YOU'RE NEEDED...

HEY?! OUCH!

GRRR

YOU! NOW'S NOT THE TIME TO MESS WITH ME! GET IT?...

SWALLOW THIS AND GET TO WORK!

BAH!

I'M LISTENING...

AT THE SUFFUSS... ONE OF MY WARRIORS BACK FROM SEEING THEM TOLD ME ABOUT MANY BAGULINS FLOCKING THERE... BAGULINS AREN'T REAL WARRIORS, JUST BONEHEADED HERD ANIMALS, THUGS FOR DOING THE DIRTY WORK. THE KIND THAT WOULD USE XOXOS COCOON-LAUNCHERS ... IF YOU SEE WHAT I MEAN...

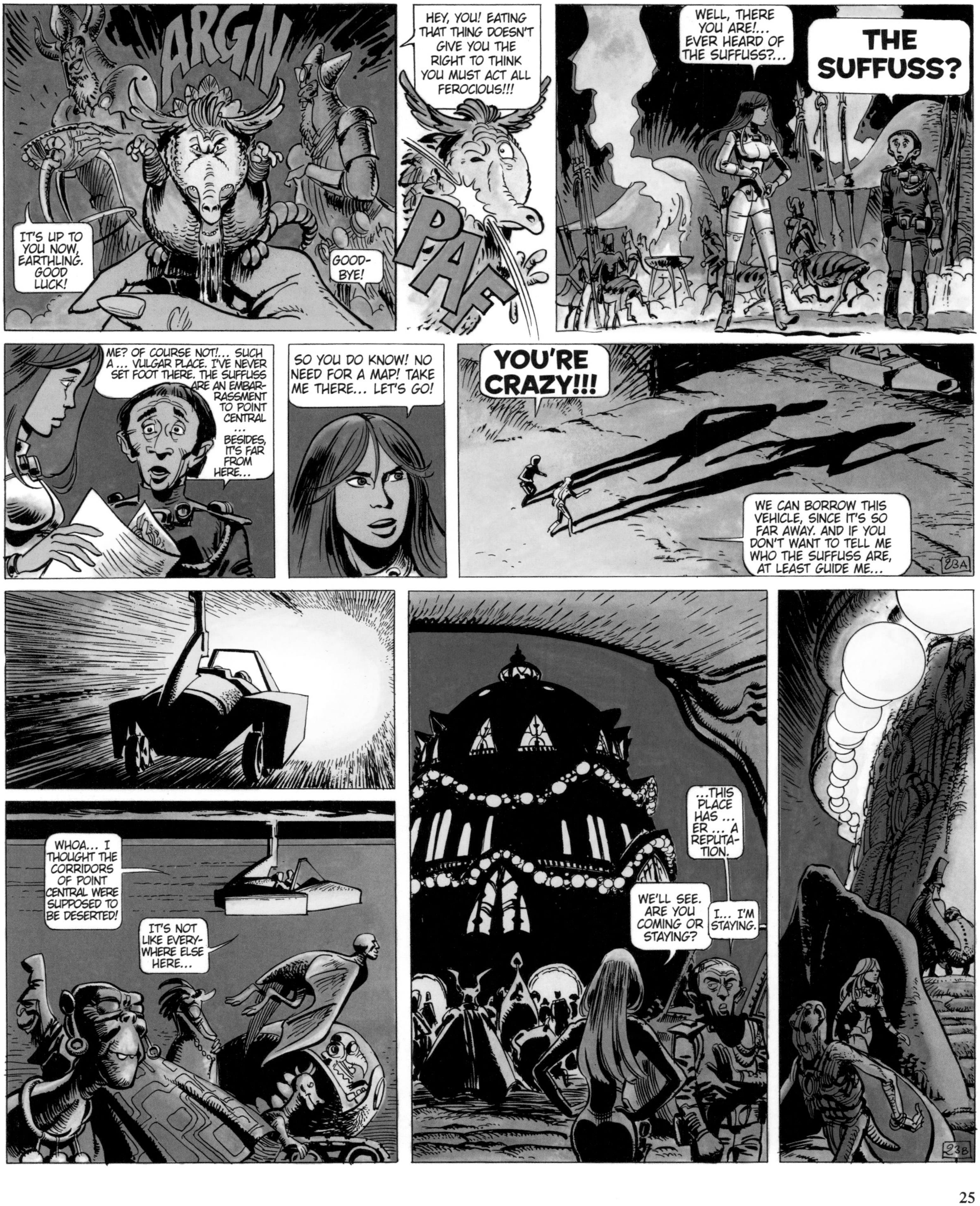
ARGN
IT'S UP TO YOU NOW, EARTHLING. GOOD LUCK!
GOOD-BYE!
HEY, YOU! EATING THAT THING DOESN'T GIVE YOU THE RIGHT TO THINK YOU MUST ACT ALL FEROCIOUS!!!
PAF
WELL, THERE YOU ARE!... EVER HEARD OF THE SUFFUSS?...
THE SUFFUSS?
ME? OF COURSE NOT!... SUCH A ... VULGAR PLACE. I'VE NEVER SET FOOT THERE. THE SUFFUSS ARE AN EMBARRASSMENT TO POINT CENTRAL ... BESIDES, IT'S FAR FROM HERE...
SO YOU DO KNOW! NO NEED FOR A MAP! TAKE ME THERE... LET'S GO!
YOU'RE CRAZY!!!
WE CAN BORROW THIS VEHICLE, SINCE IT'S SO FAR AWAY. AND IF YOU DON'T WANT TO TELL ME WHO THE SUFFUSS ARE, AT LEAST GUIDE ME...
23A
WHOA... I THOUGHT THE CORRIDORS OF POINT CENTRAL WERE SUPPOSED TO BE DESERTED!
IT'S NOT LIKE EVERYWHERE ELSE HERE...
...THIS PLACE HAS ... ER ... A REPUTATION.
WE'LL SEE. ARE YOU COMING OR STAYING?
I... I'M STAYING.
23B

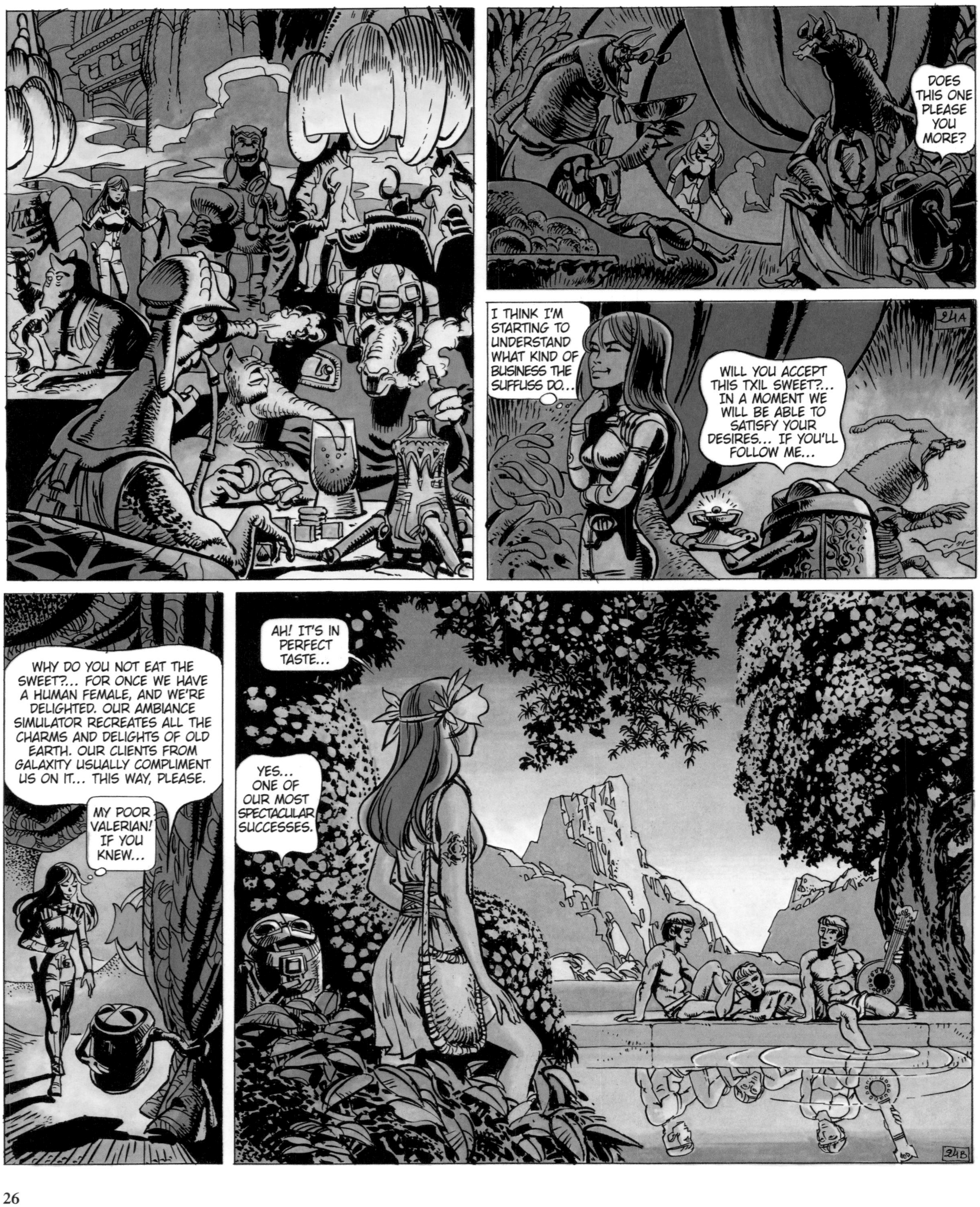
DOES THIS ONE PLEASE YOU MORE?
I THINK I'M STARTING TO UNDERSTAND WHAT KIND OF BUSINESS THE SUFFUSS DO...
24A
WILL YOU ACCEPT THIS TXIL SWEET?... IN A MOMENT WE WILL BE ABLE TO SATISFY YOUR DESIRES... IF YOU'LL FOLLOW ME...
WHY DO YOU NOT EAT THE SWEET?... FOR ONCE WE HAVE A HUMAN FEMALE, AND WE'RE DELIGHTED. OUR AMBIANCE SIMULATOR RECREATES ALL THE CHARMS AND DELIGHTS OF OLD EARTH. OUR CLIENTS FROM GALAXITY USUALLY COMPLIMENT US ON IT... THIS WAY, PLEASE.
MY POOR VALERIAN! IF YOU KNEW...
AH! IT'S IN PERFECT TASTE...
YES... ONE OF OUR MOST SPECTACULAR SUCCESSES.
24B

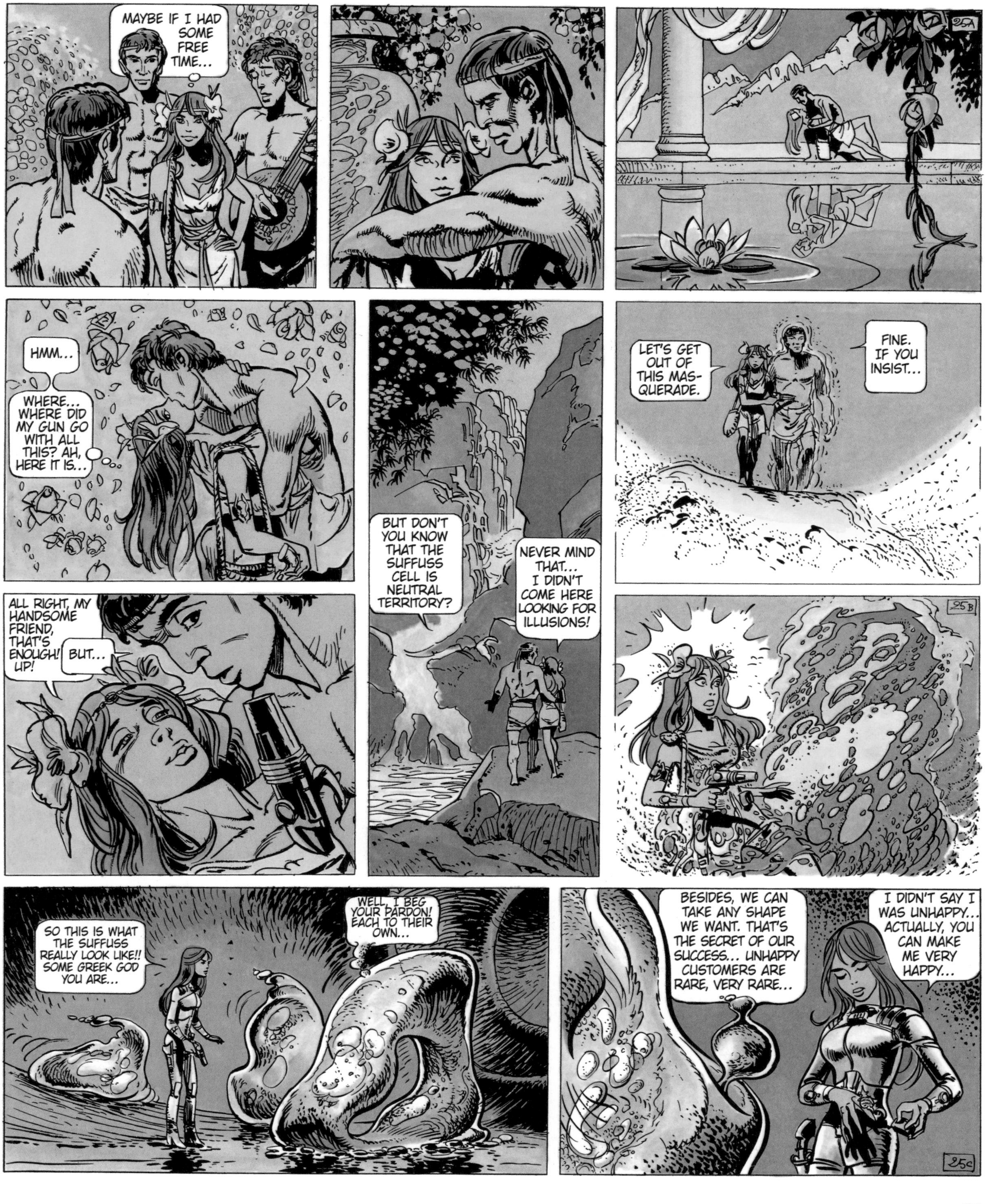
MAYBE IF I HAD SOME FREE TIME...
25A
HMM...
WHERE... WHERE DID MY GUN GO WITH ALL THIS? AH, HERE IT IS...
BUT DON'T YOU KNOW THAT THE SUFFUSS CELL IS NEUTRAL TERRITORY?
NEVER MIND THAT... I DIDN'T COME HERE LOOKING FOR ILLUSIONS!
LET'S GET OUT OF THIS MAS-QUERADE.
FINE. IF YOU INSIST...
ALL RIGHT, MY HANDSOME FRIEND, THAT'S ENOUGH! UP!
BUT...
25B
SO THIS IS WHAT THE SUFFUSS REALLY LOOK LIKE!! SOME GREEK GOD YOU ARE...
WELL, I BEG YOUR PARDON! EACH TO THEIR OWN...
BESIDES, WE CAN TAKE ANY SHAPE WE WANT. THAT'S THE SECRET OF OUR SUCCESS... UNHAPPY CUSTOMERS ARE RARE, VERY RARE...
I DIDN'T SAY I WAS UNHAPPY... ACTUALLY, YOU CAN MAKE ME VERY HAPPY...
25C

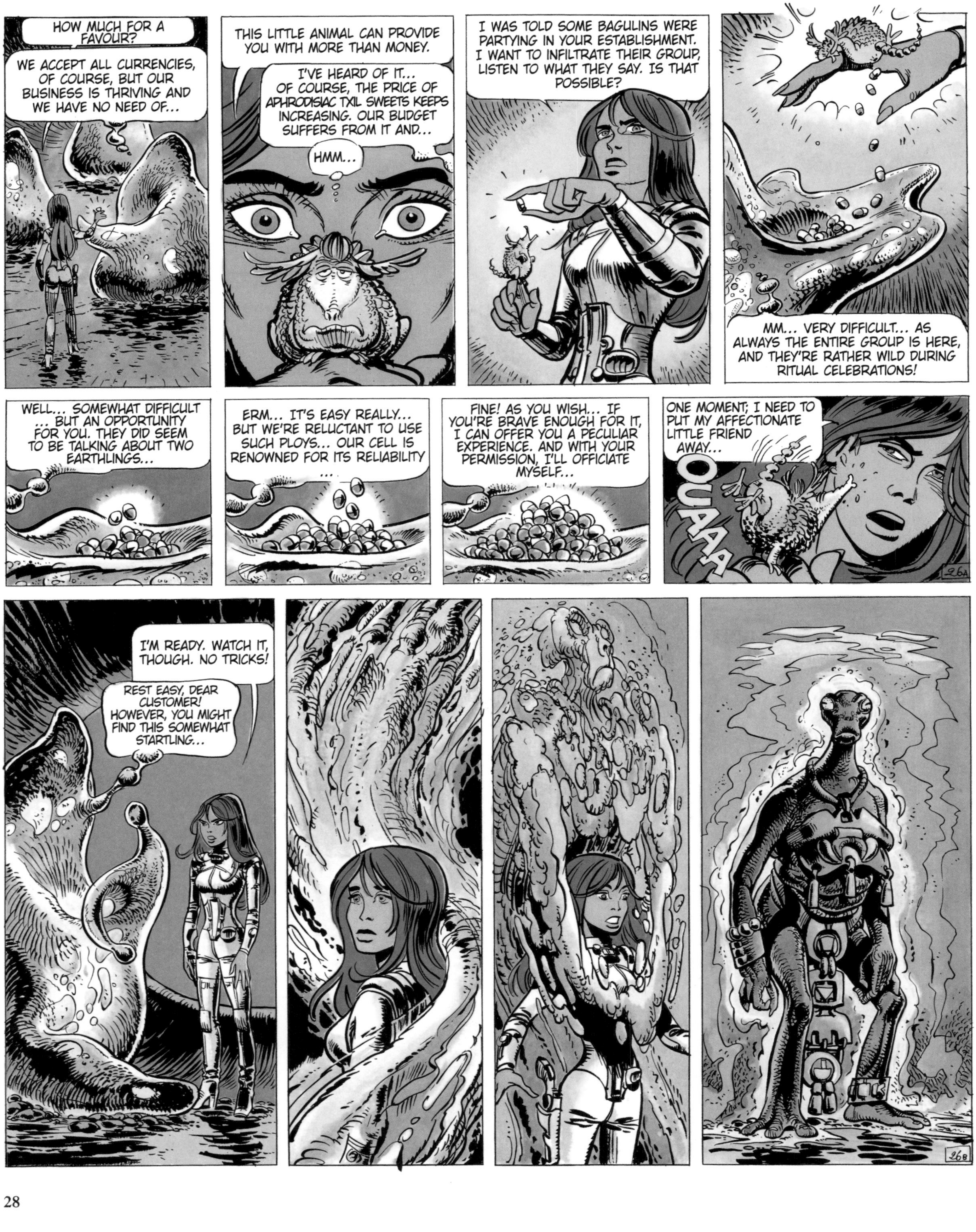
HOW MUCH FOR A FAVOUR?
WE ACCEPT ALL CURRENCIES, OF COURSE, BUT OUR BUSINESS IS THRIVING AND WE HAVE NO NEED OF...
THIS LITTLE ANIMAL CAN PROVIDE YOU WITH MORE THAN MONEY.
I'VE HEARD OF IT... OF COURSE, THE PRICE OF APHRODISIAC TXIL SWEETS KEEPS INCREASING. OUR BUDGET SUFFERS FROM IT AND...
HMM...
I WAS TOLD SOME BAGULINS WERE PARTYING IN YOUR ESTABLISHMENT. I WANT TO INFILTRATE THEIR GROUP, LISTEN TO WHAT THEY SAY. IS THAT POSSIBLE?
MM... VERY DIFFICULT... AS ALWAYS THE ENTIRE GROUP IS HERE, AND THEY'RE RATHER WILD DURING RITUAL CELEBRATIONS!
WELL... SOMEWHAT DIFFICULT ... BUT AN OPPORTUNITY FOR YOU. THEY DID SEEM TO BE TALKING ABOUT TWO EARTHLINGS...
ERM... IT'S EASY REALLY... BUT WE'RE RELUCTANT TO USE SUCH PLOYS... OUR CELL IS RENOWNED FOR ITS RELIABILITY ...
FINE! AS YOU WISH... IF YOU'RE BRAVE ENOUGH FOR IT, I CAN OFFER YOU A PECULIAR EXPERIENCE. AND WITH YOUR PERMISSION, I'LL OFFICIATE MYSELF...
ONE MOMENT; I NEED TO PUT MY AFFECTIONATE LITTLE FRIEND AWAY...
OUAAA
26A
I'M READY. WATCH IT, THOUGH. NO TRICKS!
REST EASY, DEAR CUSTOMER! HOWEVER, YOU MIGHT FIND THIS SOMEWHAT STARTLING...
26B

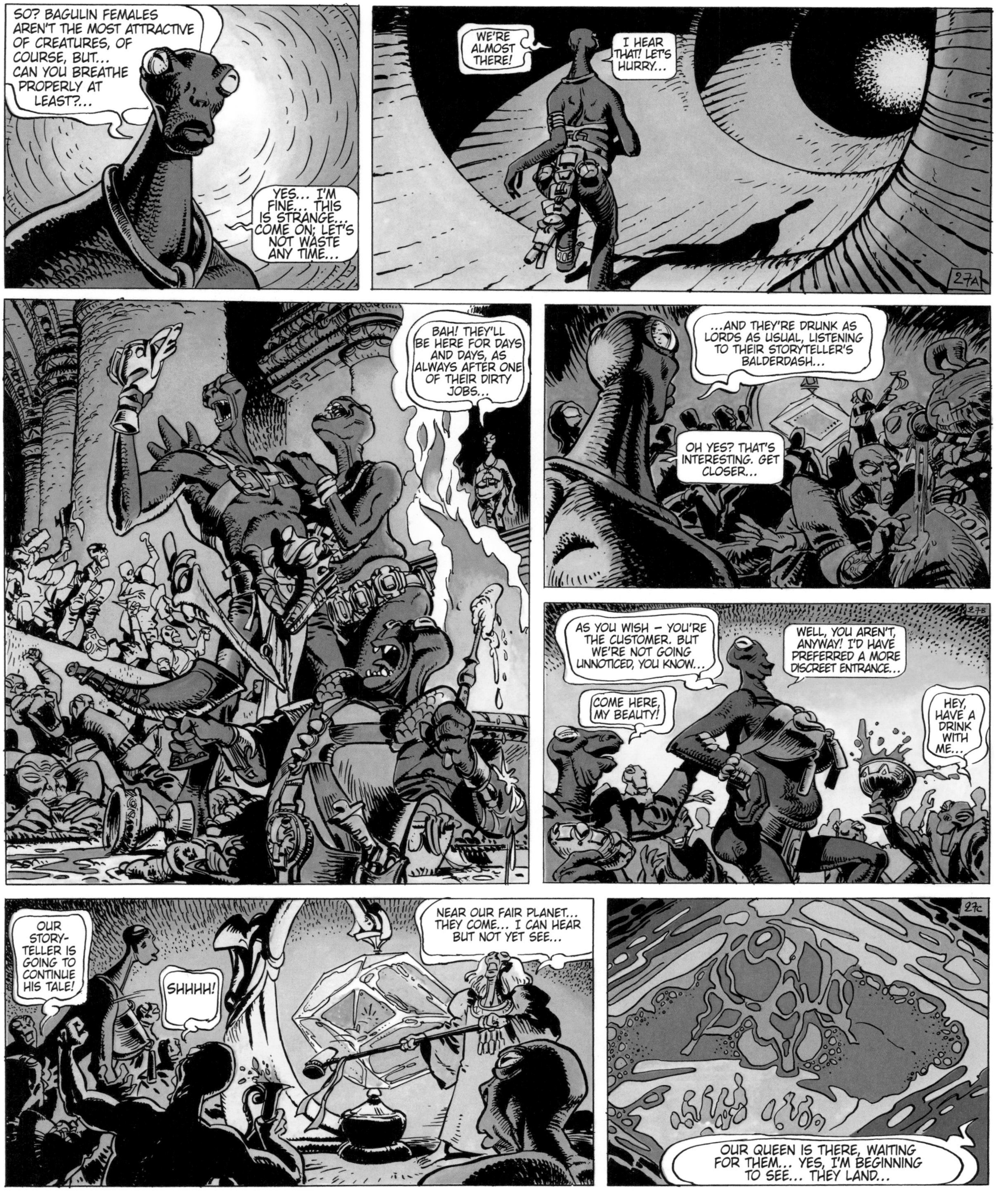
SO? BAGULIN FEMALES AREN'T THE MOST ATTRACTIVE OF CREATURES, OF COURSE, BUT... CAN YOU BREATHE PROPERLY AT LEAST?...
YES... I'M FINE... THIS IS STRANGE... COME ON; LET'S NOT WASTE ANY TIME...
WE'RE ALMOST THERE!
I HEAR THAT! LET'S HURRY...
27A
BAH! THEY'LL BE HERE FOR DAYS AND DAYS, AS ALWAYS AFTER ONE OF THEIR DIRTY JOBS...
...AND THEY'RE DRUNK AS LORDS AS USUAL, LISTENING TO THEIR STORYTELLER'S BALDERDASH...
OH YES? THAT'S INTERESTING. GET CLOSER...
27B
AS YOU WISH – YOU'RE THE CUSTOMER. BUT WE'RE NOT GOING UNNOTICED, YOU KNOW...
WELL, YOU AREN'T, ANYWAY! I'D HAVE PREFERRED A MORE DISCREET ENTRANCE...
COME HERE, MY BEAUTY!
HEY, HAVE A DRINK WITH ME...
OUR STORY-TELLER IS GOING TO CONTINUE HIS TALE!
SHHHH!
NEAR OUR FAIR PLANET... THEY COME... I CAN HEAR BUT NOT YET SEE...
27C
OUR QUEEN IS THERE, WAITING FOR THEM... YES, I'M BEGINNING TO SEE... THEY LAND...

THEY COME OUT AND OUR QUEEN IS SATISFIED...

...BUT ONE OF THEM IS SUPERFLUOUS... SHOULD HE BE STRICKEN DEAD?

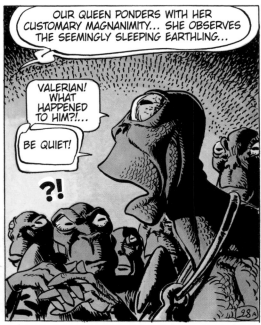

OUR QUEEN PONDERS WITH HER CUSTOMARY MAGNANIMITY... SHE OBSERVES THE SEEMINGLY SLEEPING EARTHLING...

VALERIAN! WHAT HAPPENED TO HIM?!...

BE QUIET!

?!

TIME IS SHORT, FOR IN THE LAKE OF FRAGRANT WATERS...

...THE GROOBOS WAIT TO GO WHERE THEY MUST...

OUR QUEEN HAS MADE HER DECISION: THE EXTRA MAN'S LIFE IS SPARED...

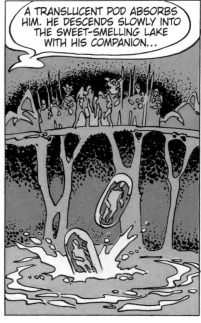

A TRANSLUCENT POD ABSORBS HIM. HE DESCENDS SLOWLY INTO THE SWEET-SMELLING LAKE WITH HIS COMPANION...

OUR BELOVED QUEEN CONGRATULATES THE HEROES. AND THE LAKE PARTS TO LET THE GROOBOS AND THEIR BURDEN DEPART.

VICTORY!!!

DRINKS !!!

COME 'ERE, GORGEOUS... LET'S CELEBRATE!!

BUT...

LET'S CLEAR OFF!

WHERE YA GOING?

BE RIGHT BACK! BE RIGHT BACK!!

HEYYY... STAY!

GET ME OUT OF HERE!!!

PHEW!

THOSE GROOBOS ... WHO ARE THEY?

HEY! THAT WASN'T PART OF OUR DEAL...

TRUE! I'M STARTING TO GRASP HOW THINGS WORK ON POINT CENTRAL...

SO?...

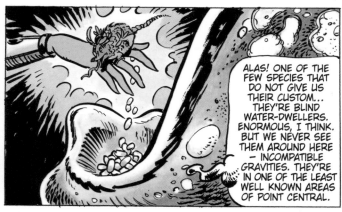

ALAS! ONE OF THE FEW SPECIES THAT DO NOT GIVE US THEIR CUSTOM... THEY'RE BLIND WATER-DWELLERS. ENORMOUS, I THINK. BUT WE NEVER SEE THEM AROUND HERE – INCOMPATIBLE GRAVITIES. THEY'RE IN ONE OF THE LEAST WELL KNOWN AREAS OF POINT CENTRAL.

THANKS ANYWAY, SUFFUSS... NO NEED TO ACCOMPANY ME OUT. I'LL FIND MY OWN WAY... HEY NOW, GRUMPY! YOU'RE A BIT OVEREXCITED AFTER ALL THOSE SWEETS, AREN'T YOU?!...

SMACK SMACK SMACK

WELL, COLONEL PROTOCOL! YOU, HERE?... I THOUGHT YOU DIDN'T FREQUENT SUCH DENS OF INIQUITY?...

ER... WELL, IT'S JUST...

YES, I KNOW... MEN FAR FROM MOTHER EARTH HAVE NEEDS, EH?...

NO NEED TO EXAGGERATE...

COME ALONG, WE'RE OUT OF HERE.

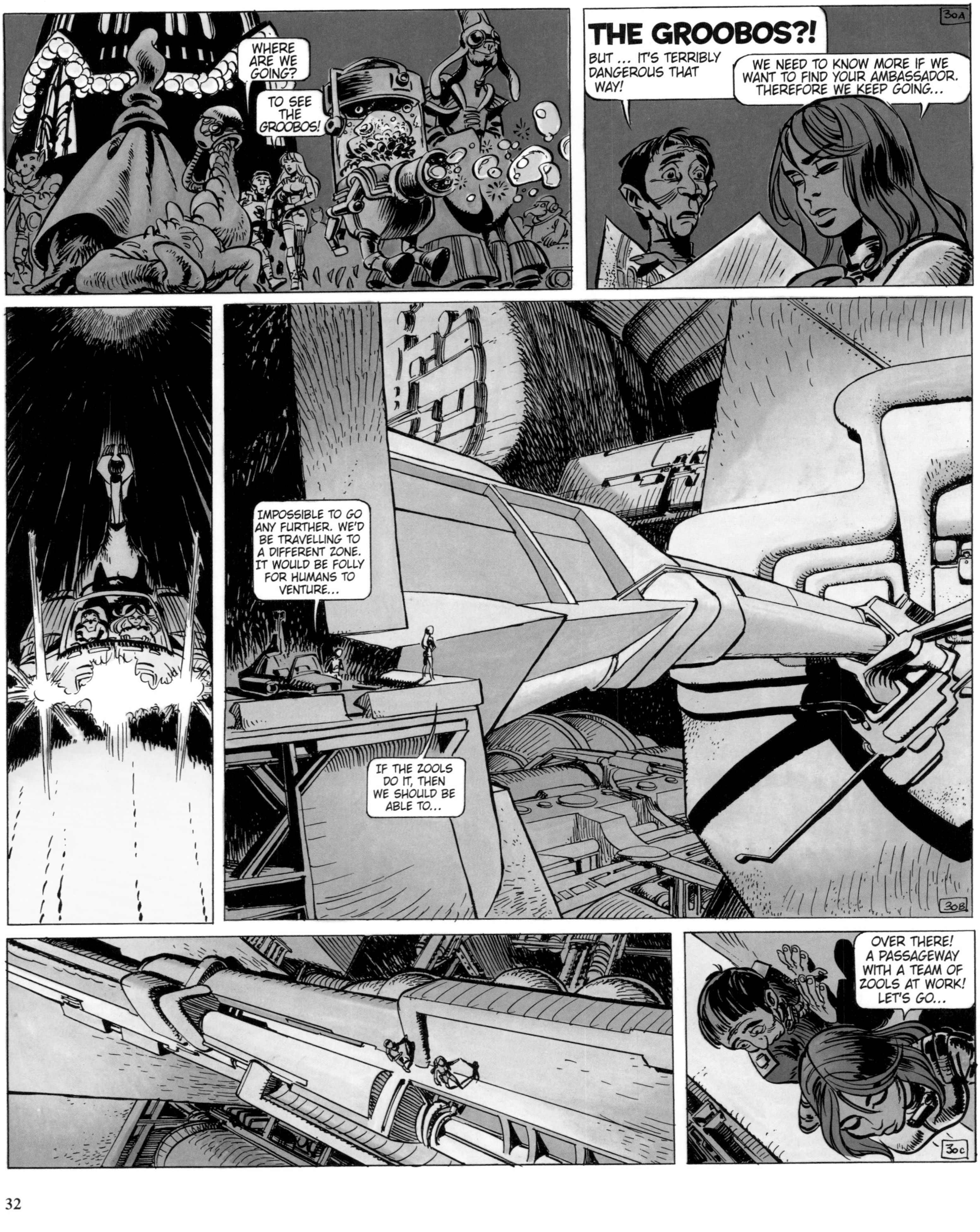
WHERE ARE WE GOING?
TO SEE THE GROOBOS!
THE GROOBOS?!
BUT ... IT'S TERRIBLY DANGEROUS THAT WAY!
WE NEED TO KNOW MORE IF WE WANT TO FIND YOUR AMBASSADOR. THEREFORE WE KEEP GOING...
30A
IMPOSSIBLE TO GO ANY FURTHER. WE'D BE TRAVELLING TO A DIFFERENT ZONE. IT WOULD BE FOLLY FOR HUMANS TO VENTURE...
IF THE ZOOLS DO IT, THEN WE SHOULD BE ABLE TO...
30B
OVER THERE! A PASSAGEWAY WITH A TEAM OF ZOOLS AT WORK! LET'S GO...
30C

THEY REALLY AREN'T VERY INQUISITIVE... **HEY!** DO YOU KNOW HOW WE CAN CONTACT THE GROOBOS?...

PFFF... LEAVE IT. THEY WON'T ANSWER!

CLICK
EARTHLINGS!

OH, IT'S YOU AGAIN!... TREASURY RUNNING LOW?

IN A WAY... A LITTLE TITBIT ABOUT THE GROOBOS?

...FOR 1,000 EBEBE PEARLS CASH, A MEANS OF KNOWING WHAT GOES ON IN THEIR UNIQUE MINDS...

HOW AM I SUPPOSED TO PAY YOU?

YOUR CREATURE CAN, IF IT WISHES, RECONSTITUTE SOMETHING IT'S ALREADY PRODUCED, WITHOUT A NEW MODEL. BIG ENERGY EXPENDITURE, OF COURSE...

MEH!

WILL YOU BE ABLE TO DO THAT, YOU POOR THING?

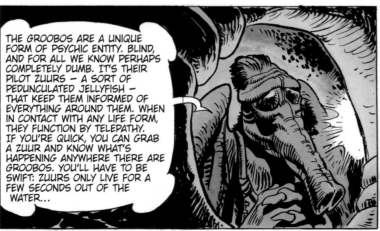

THE GROOBOS ARE A UNIQUE FORM OF PSYCHIC ENTITY. BLIND, AND FOR ALL WE KNOW PERHAPS COMPLETELY DUMB. IT'S THEIR PILOT ZUURS — A SORT OF PEDUNCULATED JELLYFISH — THAT KEEP THEM INFORMED OF EVERYTHING AROUND THEM. WHEN IN CONTACT WITH ANY LIFE FORM, THEY FUNCTION BY TELEPATHY. IF YOU'RE QUICK, YOU CAN GRAB A ZUUR AND KNOW WHAT'S HAPPENING ANYWHERE THERE ARE GROOBOS. YOU'LL HAVE TO BE SWIFT: ZUURS ONLY LIVE FOR A FEW SECONDS OUT OF THE WATER...

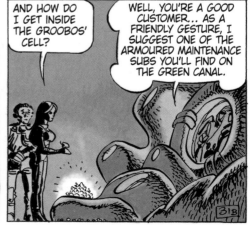

AND HOW DO I GET INSIDE THE GROOBOS' CELL?

WELL, YOU'RE A GOOD CUSTOMER... AS A FRIENDLY GESTURE, I SUGGEST ONE OF THE ARMOURED MAINTENANCE SUBS YOU'LL FIND ON THE GREEN CANAL.

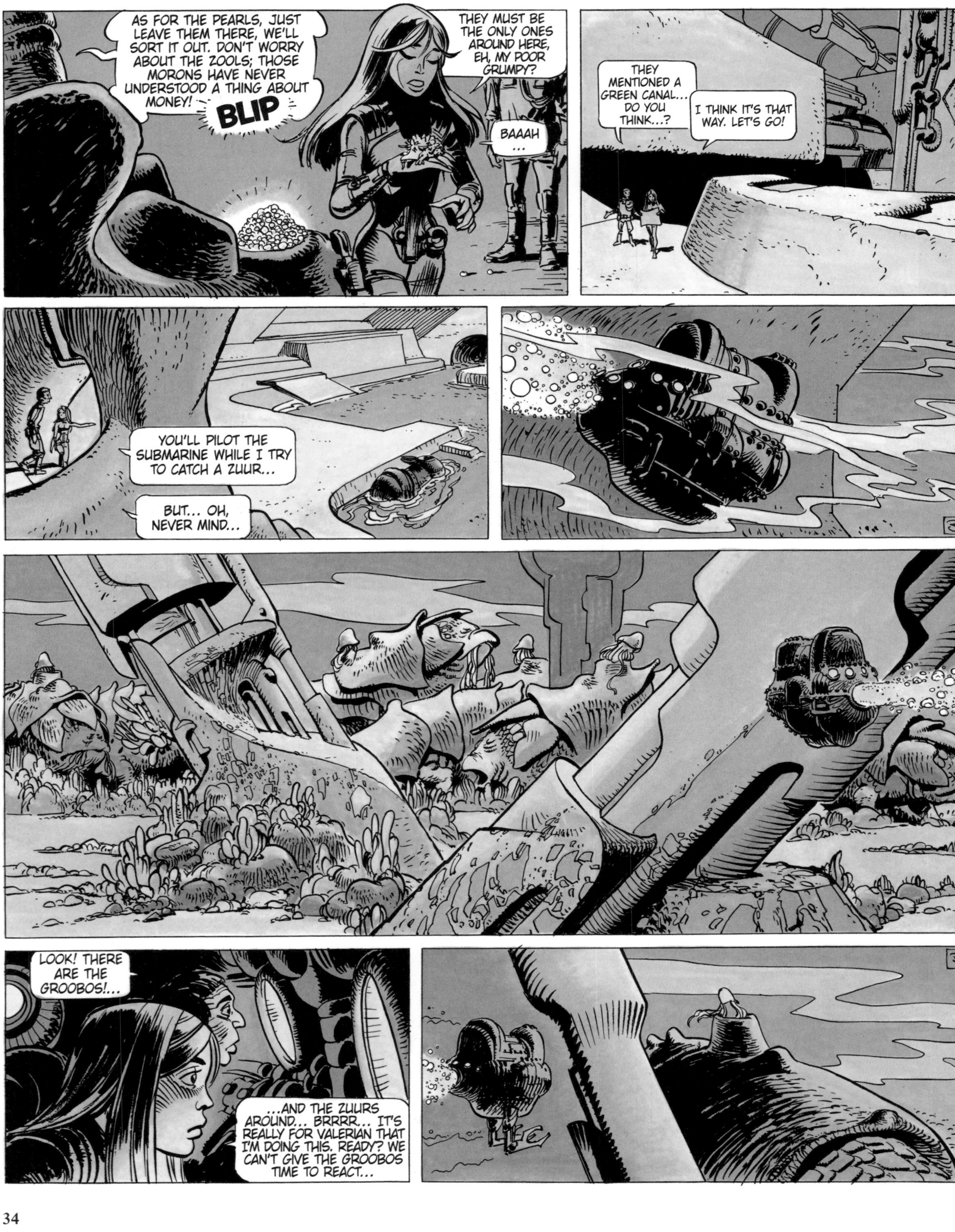
AS FOR THE PEARLS, JUST LEAVE THEM THERE, WE'LL SORT IT OUT. DON'T WORRY ABOUT THE ZOOLS; THOSE MORONS HAVE NEVER UNDERSTOOD A THING ABOUT MONEY!
BLIP
THEY MUST BE THE ONLY ONES AROUND HERE, EH, MY POOR GRUMPY?
BAAAH ...
THEY MENTIONED A GREEN CANAL... DO YOU THINK...?
I THINK IT'S THAT WAY. LET'S GO!
YOU'LL PILOT THE SUBMARINE WHILE I TRY TO CATCH A ZUUR...
BUT... OH, NEVER MIND...
32A
32B
LOOK! THERE ARE THE GROOBOS!...
...AND THE ZUURS AROUND... BRRRR... IT'S REALLY FOR VALERIAN THAT I'M DOING THIS. READY? WE CAN'T GIVE THE GROOBOS TIME TO REACT...

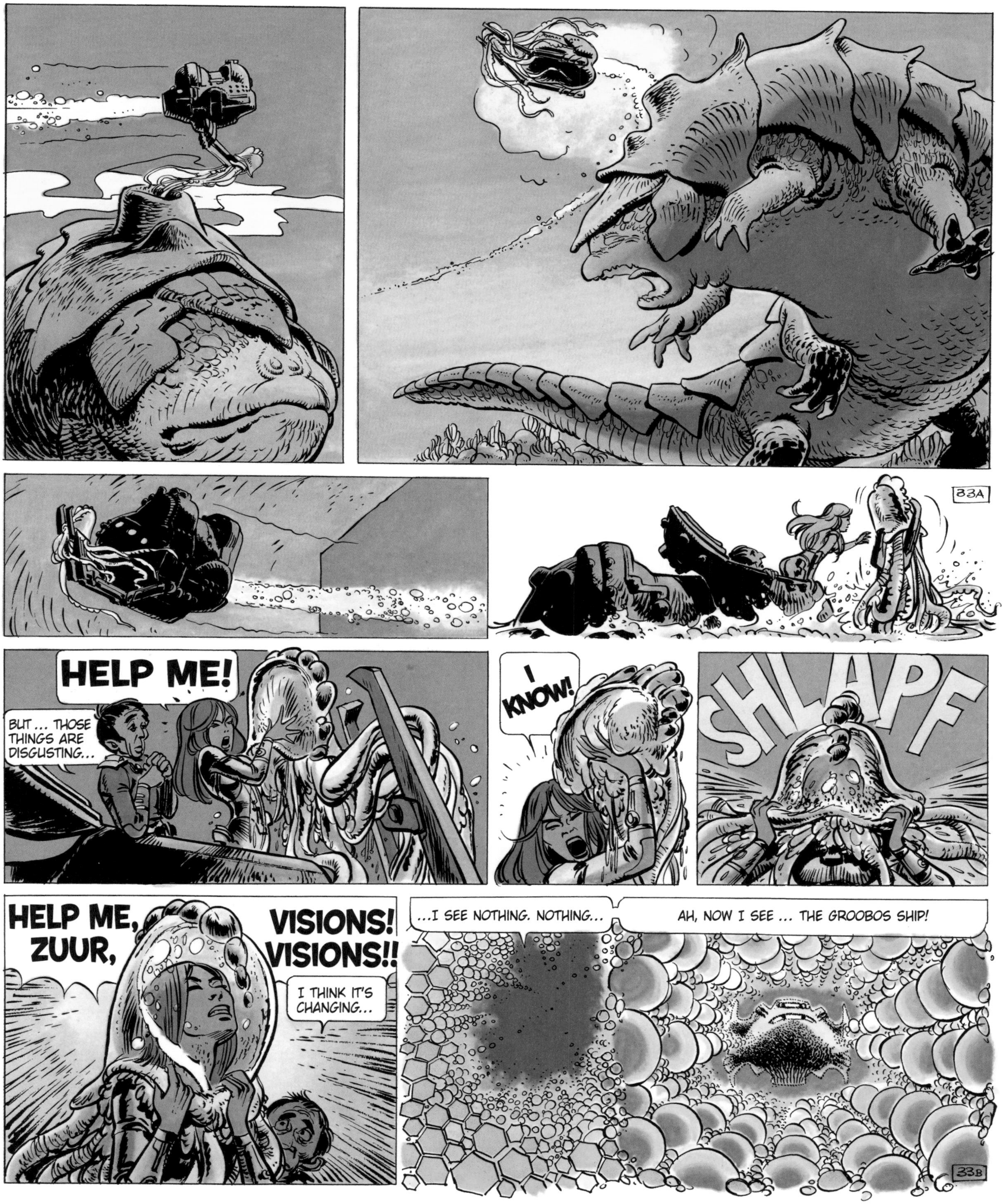
33A
HELP ME!
BUT ... THOSE THINGS ARE DISGUSTING...
I KNOW!
SHLAPF
HELP ME, ZUUR,
VISIONS! VISIONS!!
I THINK IT'S CHANGING...
...I SEE NOTHING. NOTHING...
AH, NOW I SEE ... THE GROOBOS SHIP!
33B

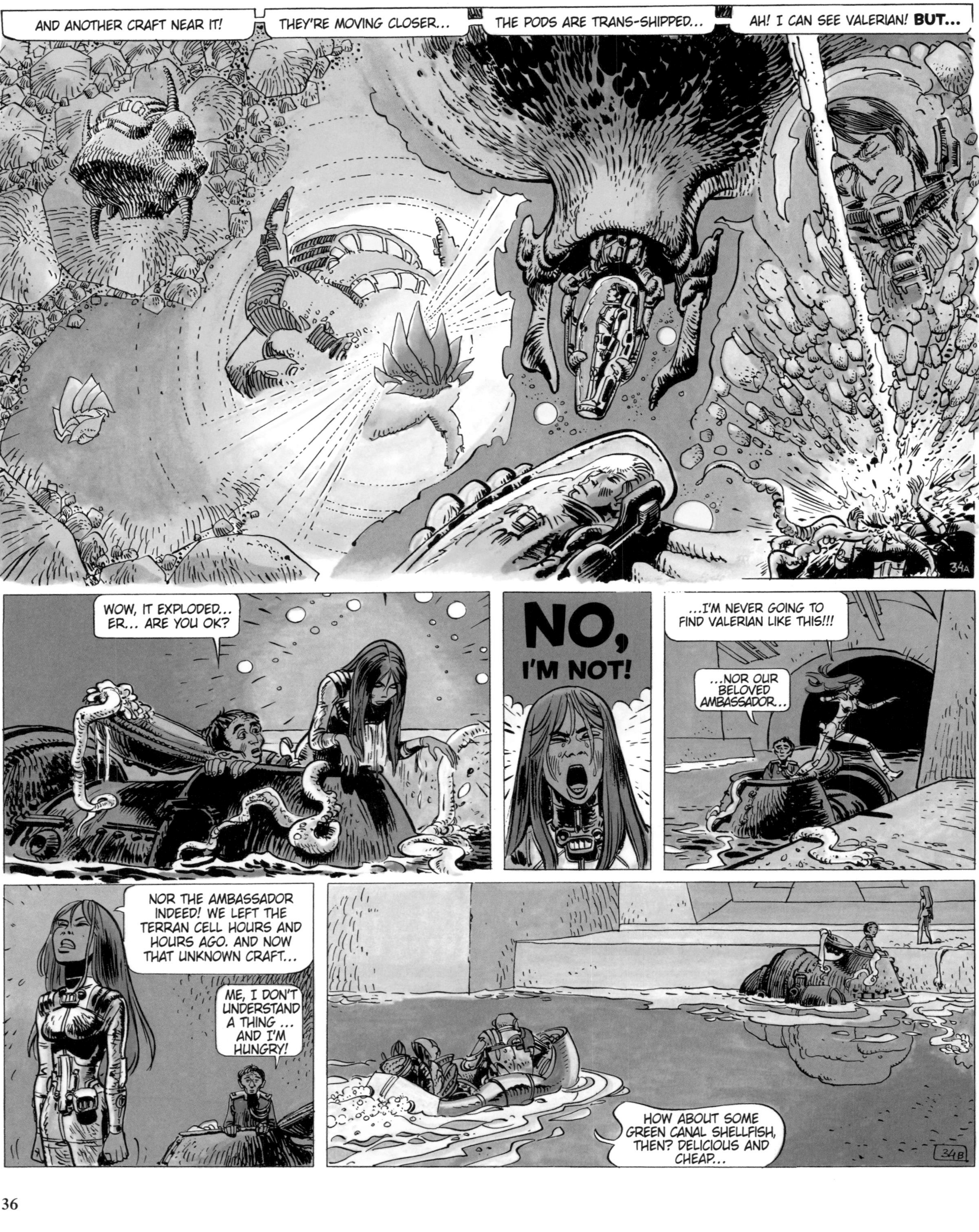
AND ANOTHER CRAFT NEAR IT!
THEY'RE MOVING CLOSER...
THE PODS ARE TRANS-SHIPPED...
AH! I CAN SEE VALERIAN! BUT...
34A
WOW, IT EXPLODED... ER... ARE YOU OK?
NO, I'M NOT!
...I'M NEVER GOING TO FIND VALERIAN LIKE THIS!!!
...NOR OUR BELOVED AMBASSADOR...
NOR THE AMBASSADOR INDEED! WE LEFT THE TERRAN CELL HOURS AND HOURS AGO. AND NOW THAT UNKNOWN CRAFT...
ME, I DON'T UNDERSTAND A THING ... AND I'M HUNGRY!
HOW ABOUT SOME GREEN CANAL SHELLFISH, THEN? DELICIOUS AND CHEAP...
34B

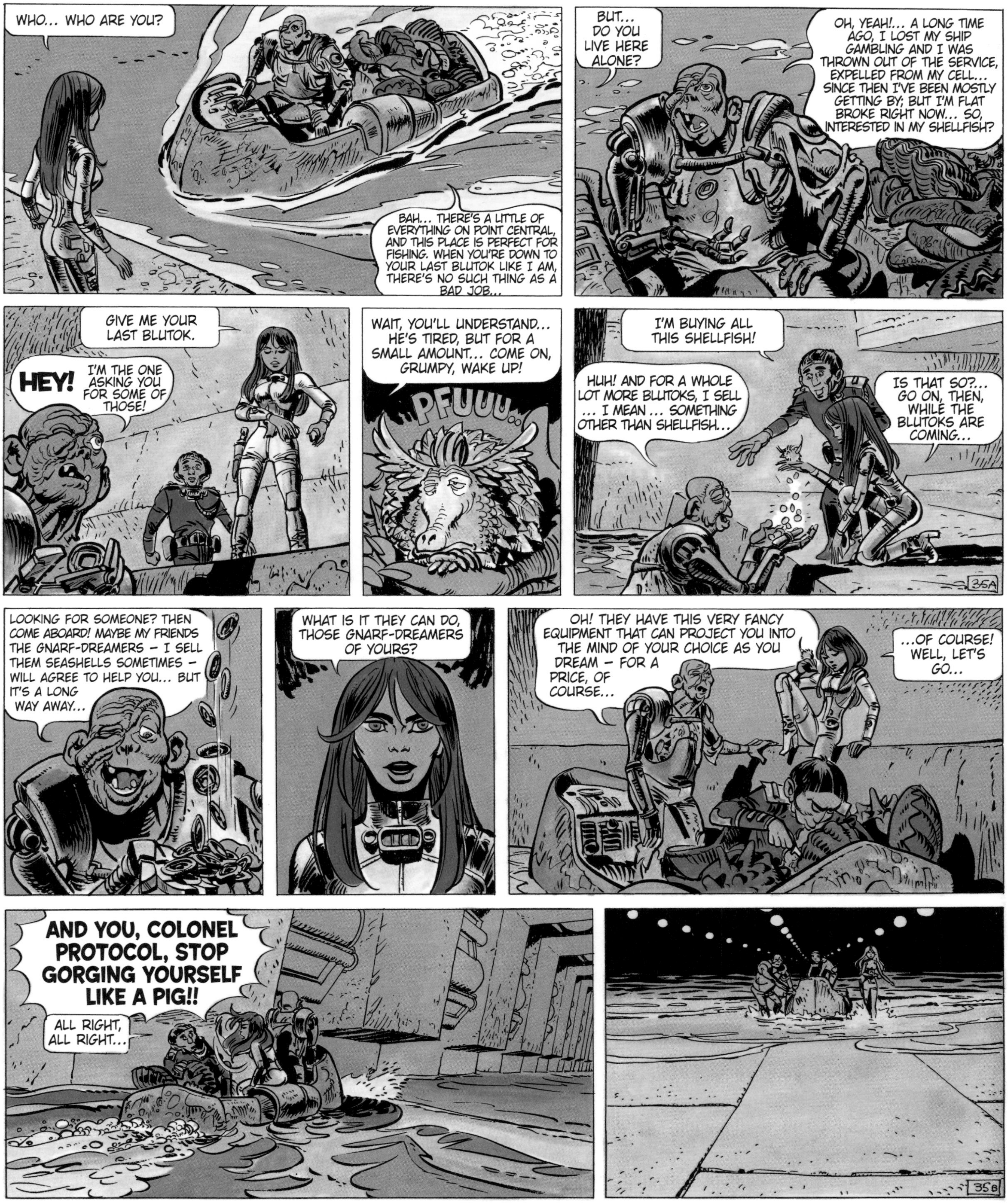
WHO... WHO ARE YOU?
BAH... THERE'S A LITTLE OF EVERYTHING ON POINT CENTRAL, AND THIS PLACE IS PERFECT FOR FISHING. WHEN YOU'RE DOWN TO YOUR LAST BLUTOK LIKE I AM, THERE'S NO SUCH THING AS A BAD JOB...
BUT... DO YOU LIVE HERE ALONE?
OH, YEAH!... A LONG TIME AGO, I LOST MY SHIP GAMBLING AND I WAS THROWN OUT OF THE SERVICE, EXPELLED FROM MY CELL... SINCE THEN I'VE BEEN MOSTLY GETTING BY; BUT I'M FLAT BROKE RIGHT NOW... SO, INTERESTED IN MY SHELLFISH?
GIVE ME YOUR LAST BLUTOK.
HEY!
I'M THE ONE ASKING YOU FOR SOME OF THOSE!
WAIT, YOU'LL UNDERSTAND... HE'S TIRED, BUT FOR A SMALL AMOUNT... COME ON, GRUMPY, WAKE UP!
PFUUU...
I'M BUYING ALL THIS SHELLFISH!
HUH! AND FOR A WHOLE LOT MORE BLUTOKS, I SELL ... I MEAN ... SOMETHING OTHER THAN SHELLFISH...
IS THAT SO?... GO ON, THEN, WHILE THE BLUTOKS ARE COMING...
35A
LOOKING FOR SOMEONE? THEN COME ABOARD! MAYBE MY FRIENDS THE GNARF-DREAMERS – I SELL THEM SEASHELLS SOMETIMES – WILL AGREE TO HELP YOU... BUT IT'S A LONG WAY AWAY...
WHAT IS IT THEY CAN DO, THOSE GNARF-DREAMERS OF YOURS?
OH! THEY HAVE THIS VERY FANCY EQUIPMENT THAT CAN PROJECT YOU INTO THE MIND OF YOUR CHOICE AS YOU DREAM – FOR A PRICE, OF COURSE...
...OF COURSE! WELL, LET'S GO...
AND YOU, COLONEL PROTOCOL, STOP GORGING YOURSELF LIKE A PIG!!
ALL RIGHT, ALL RIGHT...
35B

I BRING YOU SOMEONE INTERESTED IN YOUR TALENTS...

SO YOU HAVE BLUTOKS TO SPEND? LOTS OF BLUTOKS? WE'RE DELIGHTED TO HAVE YOU AS A CUSTOMER, PRETTY LADY...

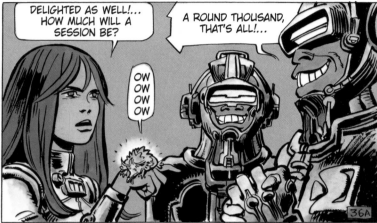

DELIGHTED AS WELL!... HOW MUCH WILL A SESSION BE?

A ROUND THOUSAND, THAT'S ALL!...

OW OW OW OW

DREAMS ARE EXPENSIVE, YOU KNOW! WE'RE CONSTANTLY IMPROVING OUR TECHNIQUES AND WE NEED TO INVEST HEAVILY. THERE'S DEPRECIATION AND OBSOLESCENCE OF EQUIPMENT, MARKETING EXPENSES AND BRANDING...

YOU SEEM RATHER ORGANISED FOR A BUNCH OF DREAMERS...

DING DILING

LET'S LEAVE YOUR ANIMAL TO ITS REMARKABLE, IF SOMEWHAT SLOW, WORK, AND ALLOW ME TO GET YOU SETTLED IN. THIS WAY...

BELIEVE ME, DREAMS ARE A SERIOUS BUSINESS THAT NEEDS TO BECOME PROFITABLE RAPIDLY. BUT I'M SURE THAT YOU'LL BE SATISFIED WITH OUR SERVICES, LIKE EVERYONE ELSE... WE INTEND TO KEEP OUR POSITION AS LEADERS IN OUR BUSINESS NICHE. THERE... JUST CONCENTRATE A LITTLE TO BEGIN AND EVERYTHING WILL BE FINE...

VALERIAN
MY SWEET VALERIAN

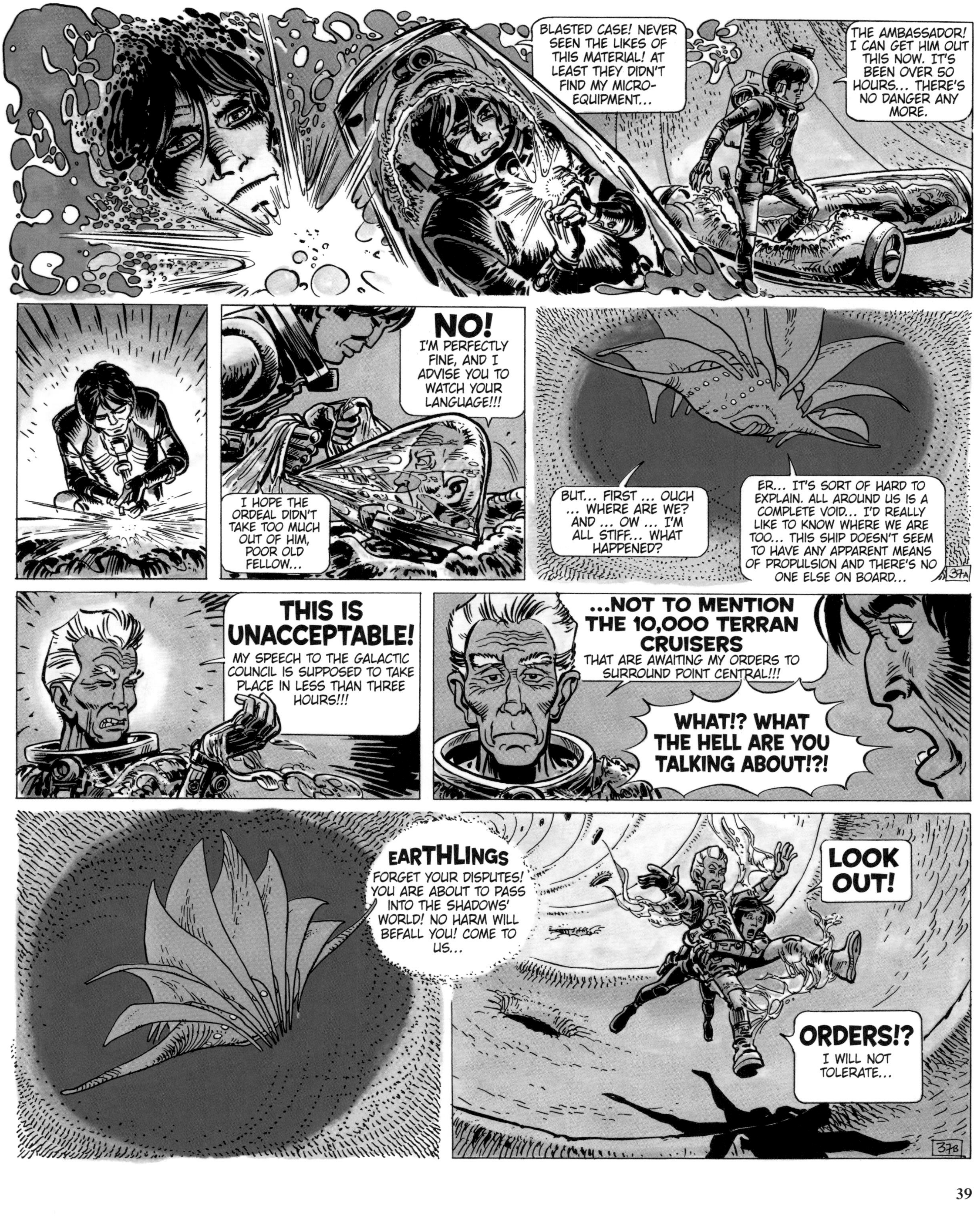
BLASTED CASE! NEVER SEEN THE LIKES OF THIS MATERIAL! AT LEAST THEY DIDN'T FIND MY MICRO-EQUIPMENT...
THE AMBASSADOR! I CAN GET HIM OUT THIS NOW. IT'S BEEN OVER 50 HOURS... THERE'S NO DANGER ANY MORE.
I HOPE THE ORDEAL DIDN'T TAKE TOO MUCH OUT OF HIM, POOR OLD FELLOW...
NO! I'M PERFECTLY FINE, AND I ADVISE YOU TO WATCH YOUR LANGUAGE!!!
BUT... FIRST ... OUCH ... WHERE ARE WE? AND ... OW ... I'M ALL STIFF... WHAT HAPPENED?
ER... IT'S SORT OF HARD TO EXPLAIN. ALL AROUND US IS A COMPLETE VOID... I'D REALLY LIKE TO KNOW WHERE WE ARE TOO... THIS SHIP DOESN'T SEEM TO HAVE ANY APPARENT MEANS OF PROPULSION AND THERE'S NO ONE ELSE ON BOARD...
37A
THIS IS UNACCEPTABLE! MY SPEECH TO THE GALACTIC COUNCIL IS SUPPOSED TO TAKE PLACE IN LESS THAN THREE HOURS!!!
...NOT TO MENTION THE 10,000 TERRAN CRUISERS THAT ARE AWAITING MY ORDERS TO SURROUND POINT CENTRAL!!!
WHAT!? WHAT THE HELL ARE YOU TALKING ABOUT!?!
EARTHLINGS FORGET YOUR DISPUTES! YOU ARE ABOUT TO PASS INTO THE SHADOWS' WORLD! NO HARM WILL BEFALL YOU! COME TO US...
LOOK OUT!
ORDERS!? I WILL NOT TOLERATE...
37B

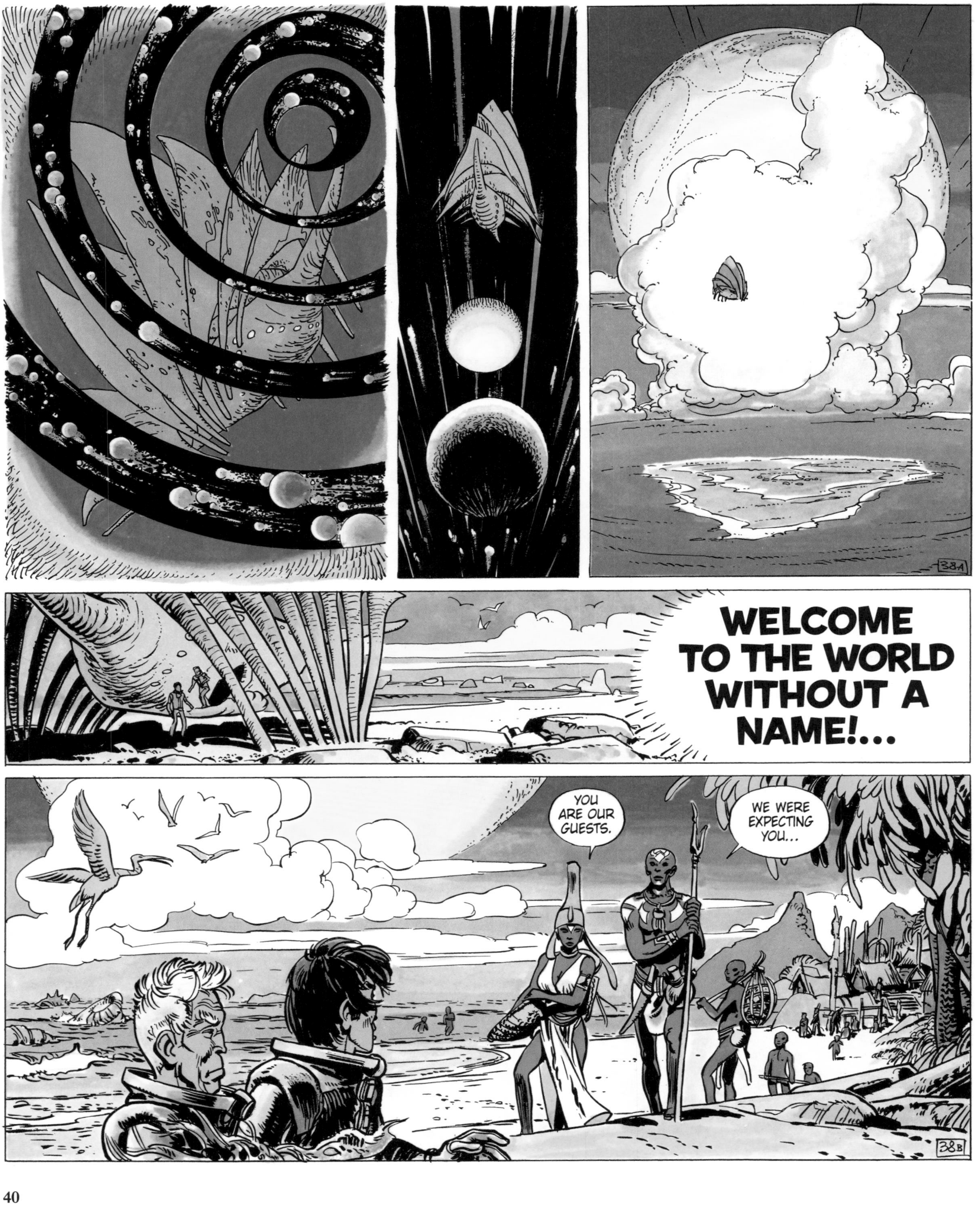
38A
WELCOME TO THE WORLD WITHOUT A NAME!...
YOU ARE OUR GUESTS.
WE WERE EXPECTING YOU...
38B

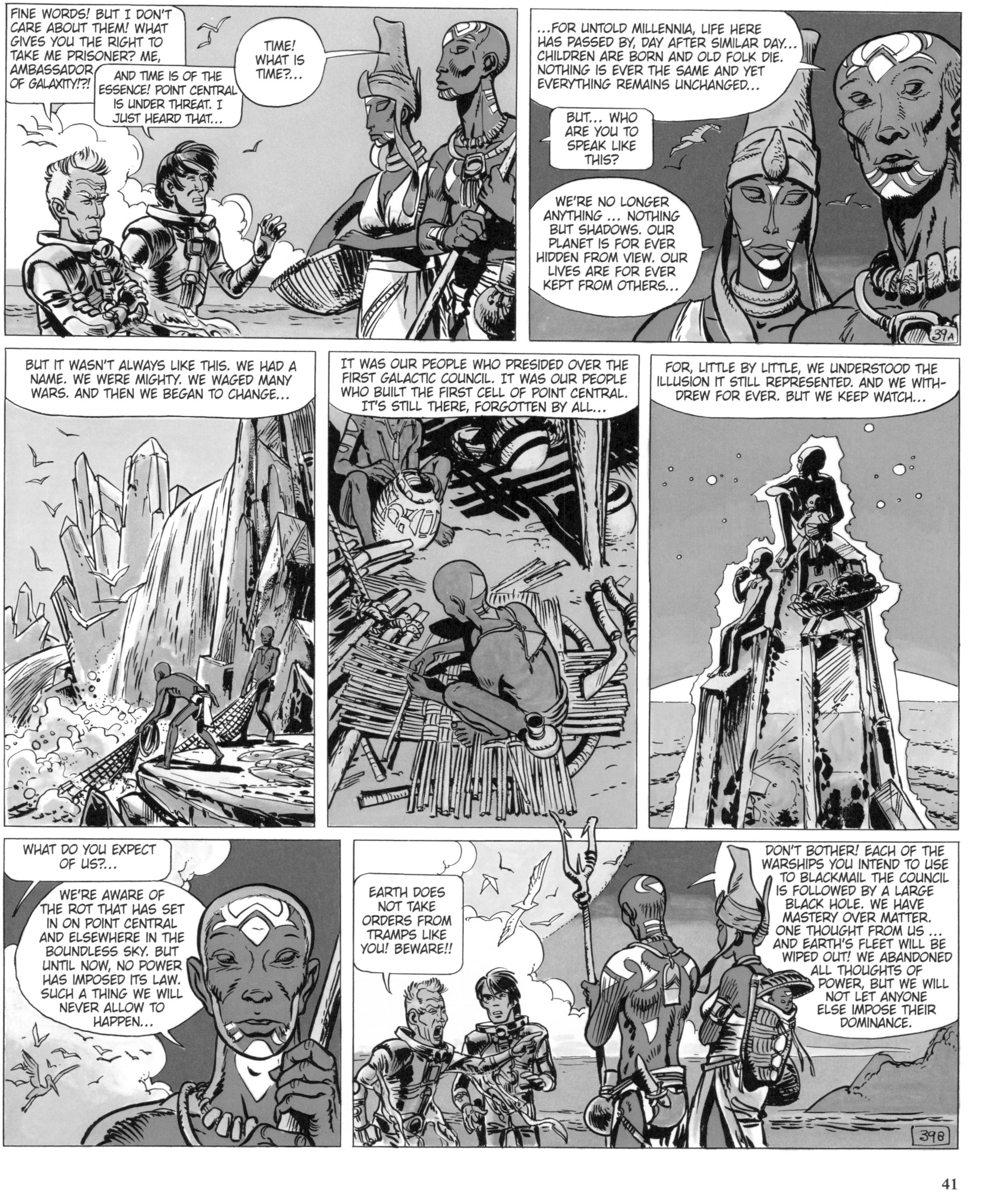
FINE WORDS! BUT I DON'T CARE ABOUT THEM! WHAT GIVES YOU THE RIGHT TO TAKE ME PRISONER? ME, AMBASSADOR OF GALAXITY!?!
AND TIME IS OF THE ESSENCE! POINT CENTRAL IS UNDER THREAT. I JUST HEARD THAT...
TIME! WHAT IS TIME?...
...FOR UNTOLD MILLENNIA, LIFE HERE HAS PASSED BY, DAY AFTER SIMILAR DAY... CHILDREN ARE BORN AND OLD FOLK DIE. NOTHING IS EVER THE SAME AND YET EVERYTHING REMAINS UNCHANGED...
BUT... WHO ARE YOU TO SPEAK LIKE THIS?
WE'RE NO LONGER ANYTHING ... NOTHING BUT SHADOWS. OUR PLANET IS FOR EVER HIDDEN FROM VIEW. OUR LIVES ARE FOR EVER KEPT FROM OTHERS...
39A
BUT IT WASN'T ALWAYS LIKE THIS. WE HAD A NAME. WE WERE MIGHTY. WE WAGED MANY WARS. AND THEN WE BEGAN TO CHANGE...
IT WAS OUR PEOPLE WHO PRESIDED OVER THE FIRST GALACTIC COUNCIL. IT WAS OUR PEOPLE WHO BUILT THE FIRST CELL OF POINT CENTRAL. IT'S STILL THERE, FORGOTTEN BY ALL...
FOR, LITTLE BY LITTLE, WE UNDERSTOOD THE ILLUSION IT STILL REPRESENTED. AND WE WITH-DREW FOR EVER. BUT WE KEEP WATCH...
WHAT DO YOU EXPECT OF US?...
WE'RE AWARE OF THE ROT THAT HAS SET IN ON POINT CENTRAL AND ELSEWHERE IN THE BOUNDLESS SKY. BUT UNTIL NOW, NO POWER HAS IMPOSED ITS LAW. SUCH A THING WE WILL NEVER ALLOW TO HAPPEN...
EARTH DOES NOT TAKE ORDERS FROM TRAMPS LIKE YOU! BEWARE!!
DON'T BOTHER! EACH OF THE WARSHIPS YOU INTEND TO USE TO BLACKMAIL THE COUNCIL IS FOLLOWED BY A LARGE BLACK HOLE. WE HAVE MASTERY OVER MATTER. ONE THOUGHT FROM US ... AND EARTH'S FLEET WILL BE WIPED OUT! WE ABANDONED ALL THOUGHTS OF POWER, BUT WE WILL NOT LET ANYONE ELSE IMPOSE THEIR DOMINANCE.
39B

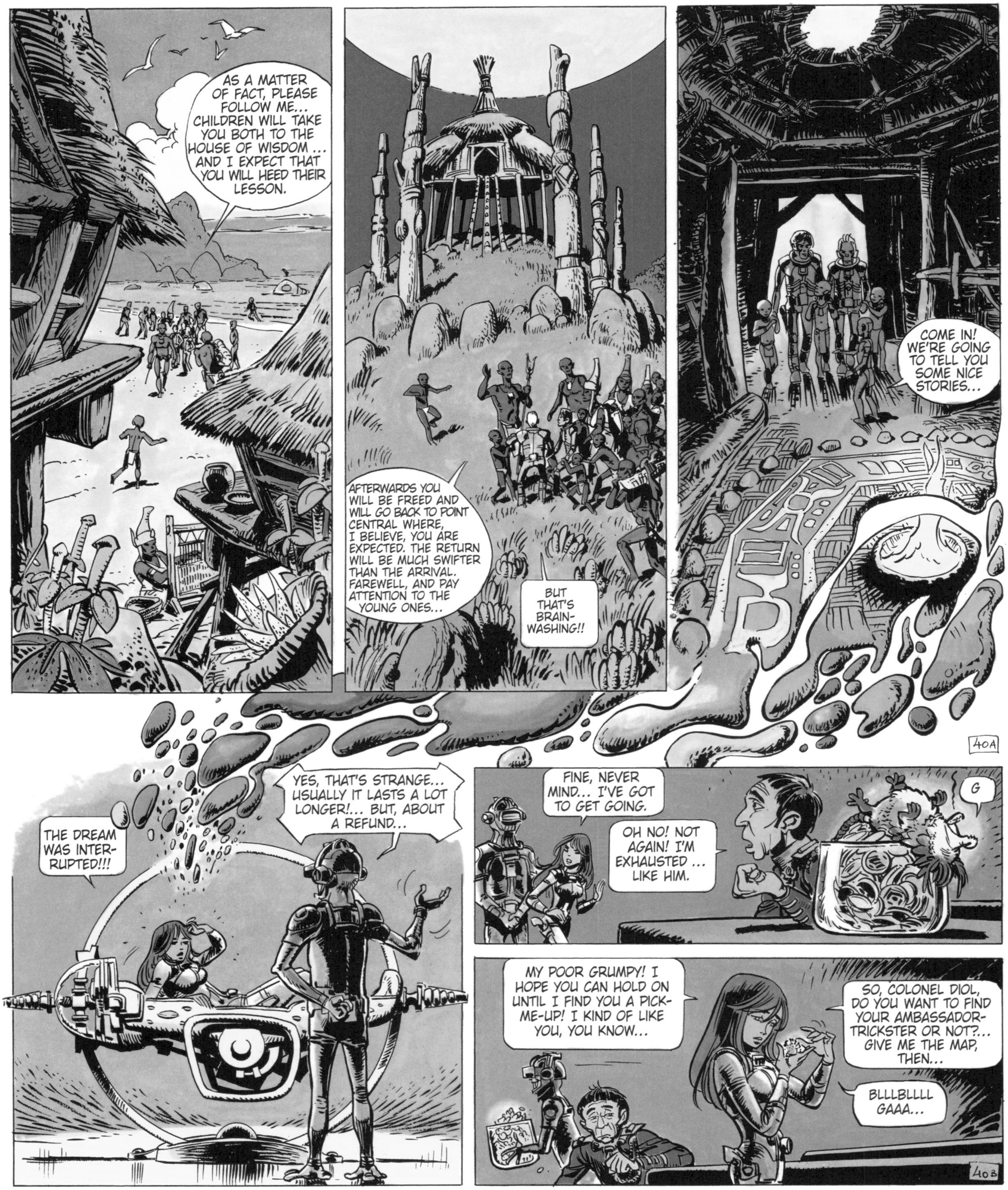
AS A MATTER OF FACT, PLEASE FOLLOW ME... CHILDREN WILL TAKE YOU BOTH TO THE HOUSE OF WISDOM ... AND I EXPECT THAT YOU WILL HEED THEIR LESSON.
AFTERWARDS YOU WILL BE FREED AND WILL GO BACK TO POINT CENTRAL WHERE, I BELIEVE, YOU ARE EXPECTED. THE RETURN WILL BE MUCH SWIFTER THAN THE ARRIVAL. FAREWELL, AND PAY ATTENTION TO THE YOUNG ONES...
BUT THAT'S BRAIN-WASHING!!
COME IN! WE'RE GOING TO TELL YOU SOME NICE STORIES...
40A
THE DREAM WAS INTER-RUPTED!!!
YES, THAT'S STRANGE... USUALLY IT LASTS A LOT LONGER!... BUT, ABOUT A REFUND...
FINE, NEVER MIND... I'VE GOT TO GET GOING.
OH NO! NOT AGAIN! I'M EXHAUSTED ... LIKE HIM.
G
MY POOR GRUMPY! I HOPE YOU CAN HOLD ON UNTIL I FIND YOU A PICK-ME-UP! I KIND OF LIKE YOU, YOU KNOW...
SO, COLONEL DIOL, DO YOU WANT TO FIND YOUR AMBASSADOR-TRICKSTER OR NOT?... GIVE ME THE MAP, THEN...
BLLLBLLLL GAAA...
40B

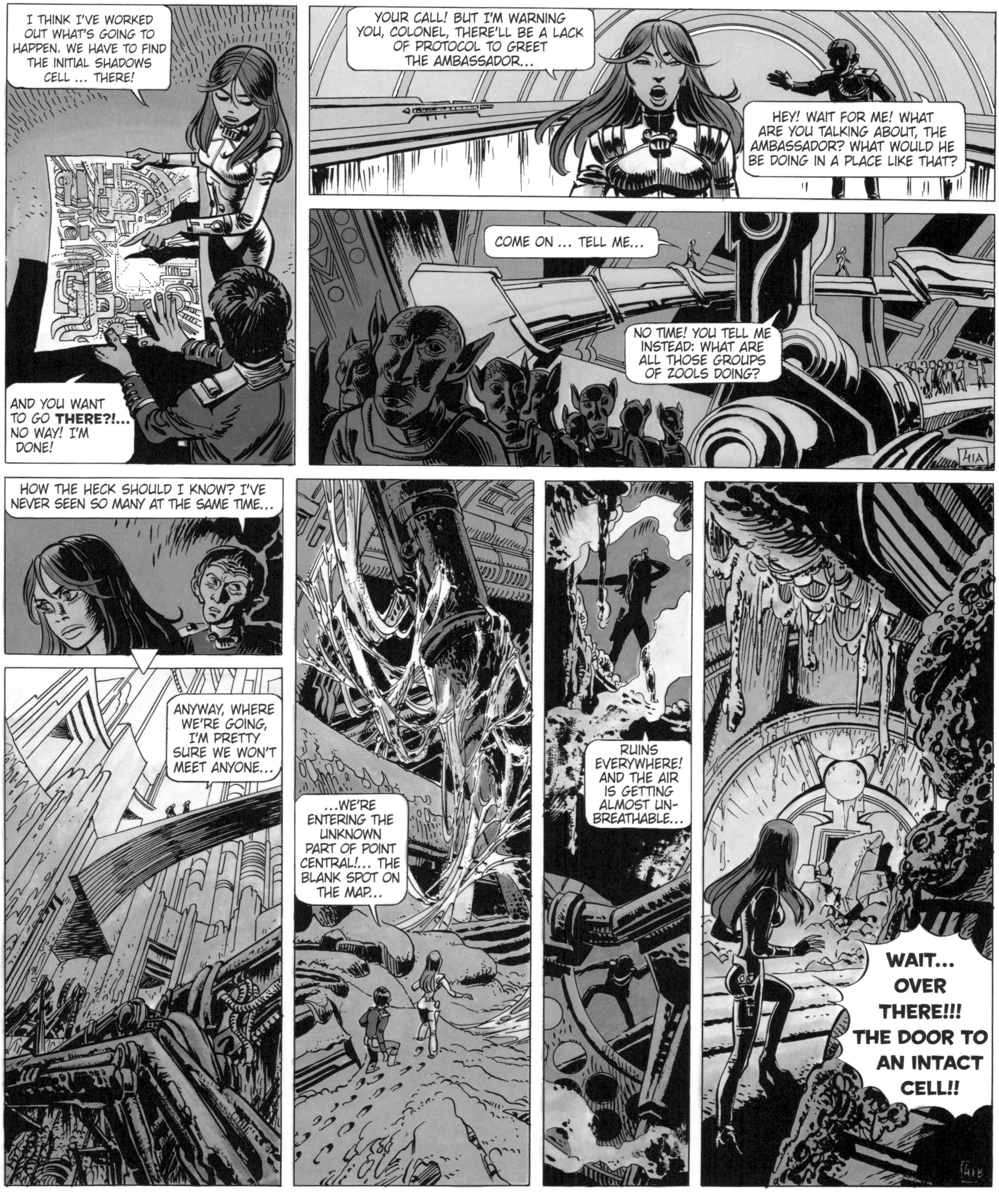
I THINK I'VE WORKED OUT WHAT'S GOING TO HAPPEN. WE HAVE TO FIND THE INITIAL SHADOWS CELL ... THERE!
AND YOU WANT TO GO **THERE?!...** NO WAY! I'M DONE!
YOUR CALL! BUT I'M WARNING YOU, COLONEL, THERE'LL BE A LACK OF PROTOCOL TO GREET THE AMBASSADOR...
HEY! WAIT FOR ME! WHAT ARE YOU TALKING ABOUT, THE AMBASSADOR? WHAT WOULD HE BE DOING IN A PLACE LIKE THAT?
COME ON ... TELL ME...
NO TIME! YOU TELL ME INSTEAD: WHAT ARE ALL THOSE GROUPS OF ZOOLS DOING?
41A
HOW THE HECK SHOULD I KNOW? I'VE NEVER SEEN SO MANY AT THE SAME TIME...
ANYWAY, WHERE WE'RE GOING, I'M PRETTY SURE WE WON'T MEET ANYONE...
...WE'RE ENTERING THE UNKNOWN PART OF POINT CENTRAL!... THE BLANK SPOT ON THE MAP...
RUINS EVERYWHERE! AND THE AIR IS GETTING ALMOST UN-BREATHABLE...
WAIT... OVER THERE!!! THE DOOR TO AN INTACT CELL!!
41B

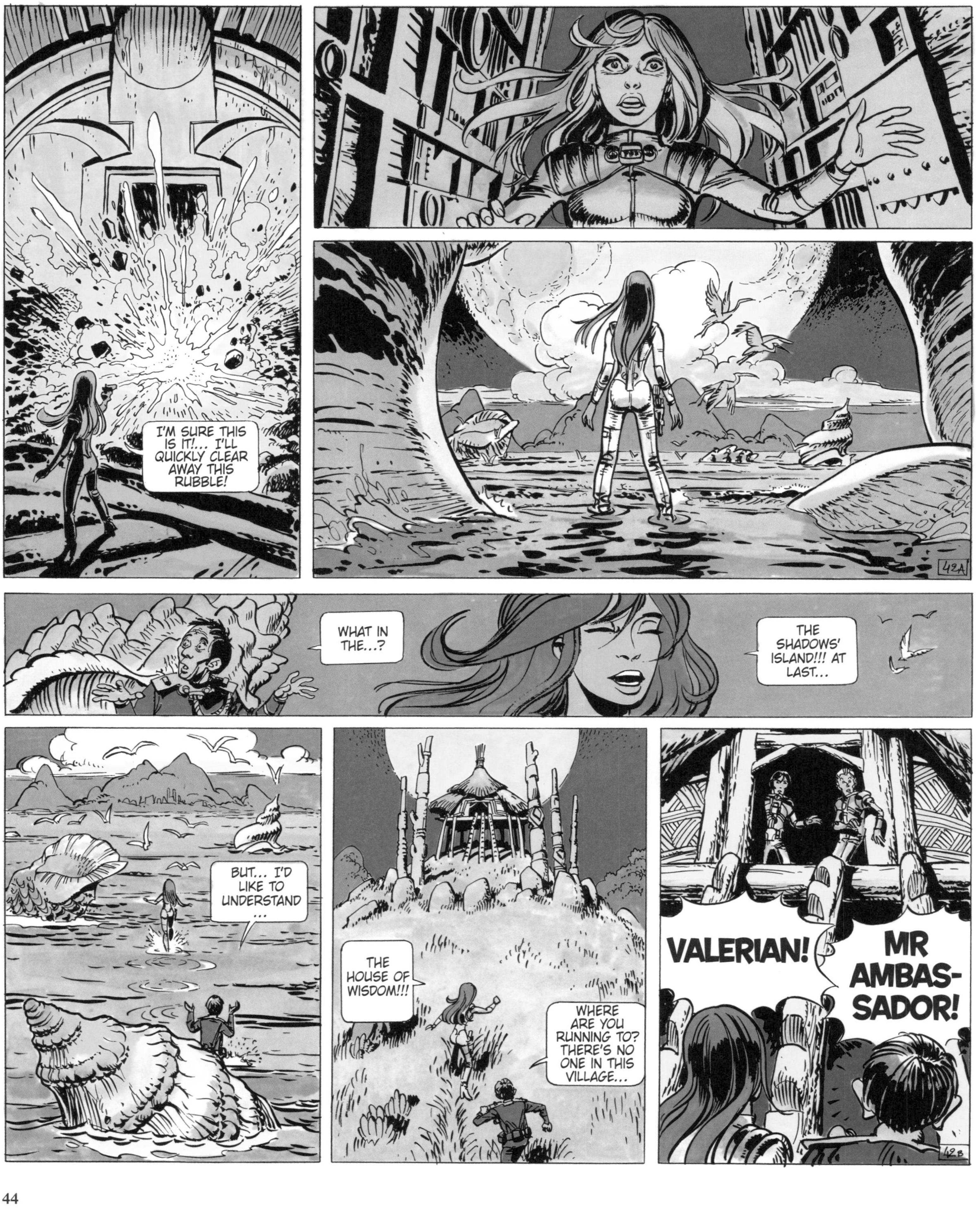
I'M SURE THIS IS IT!... I'LL QUICKLY CLEAR AWAY THIS RUBBLE!
42A
WHAT IN THE...?
THE SHADOWS' ISLAND!!! AT LAST...
BUT... I'D LIKE TO UNDERSTAND ...
THE HOUSE OF WISDOM!!!
WHERE ARE YOU RUNNING TO? THERE'S NO ONE IN THIS VILLAGE...
VALERIAN!
MR AMBASSADOR!
42B

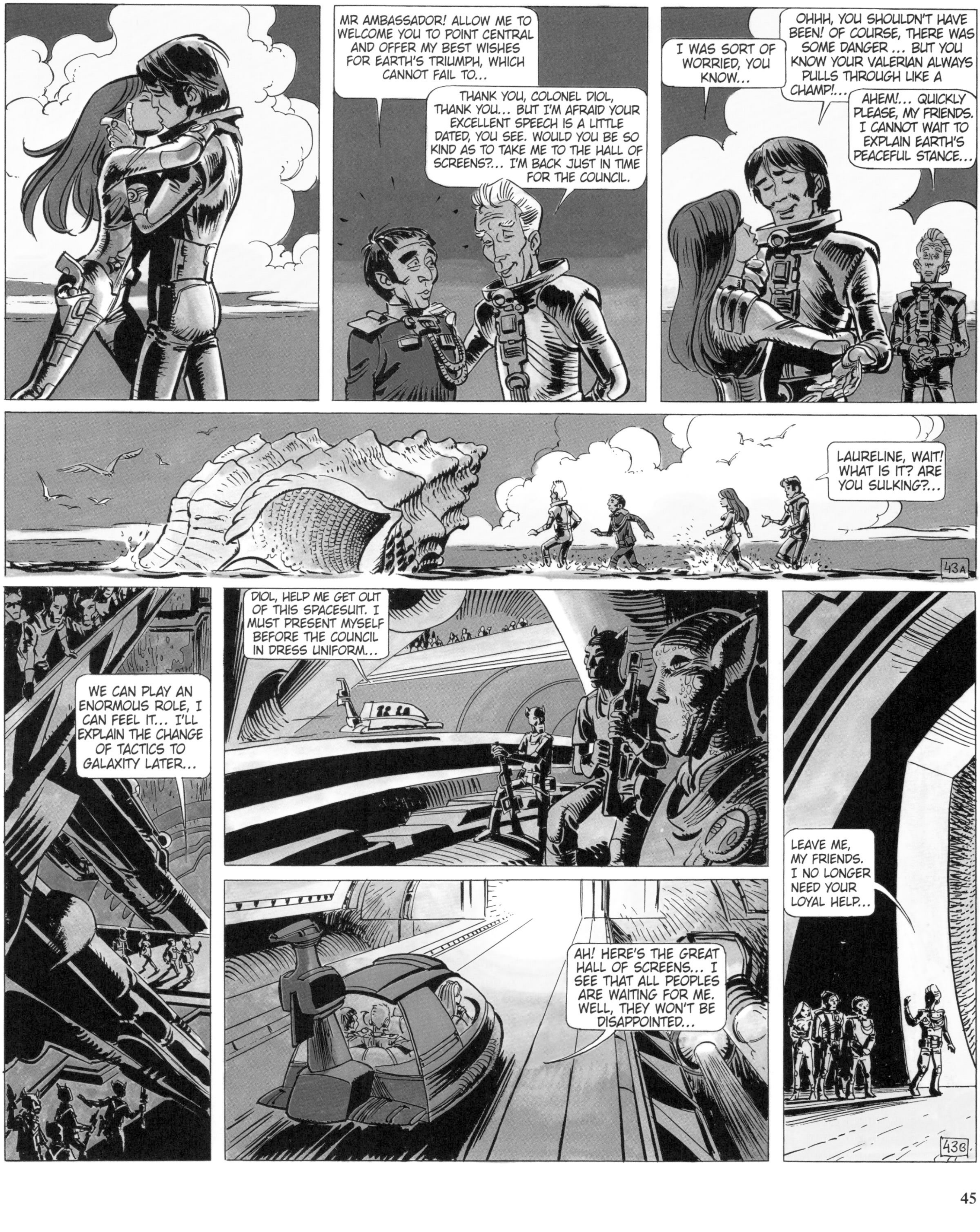
MR AMBASSADOR! ALLOW ME TO WELCOME YOU TO POINT CENTRAL AND OFFER MY BEST WISHES FOR EARTH'S TRIUMPH, WHICH CANNOT FAIL TO...
THANK YOU, COLONEL DIOL, THANK YOU... BUT I'M AFRAID YOUR EXCELLENT SPEECH IS A LITTLE DATED, YOU SEE. WOULD YOU BE SO KIND AS TO TAKE ME TO THE HALL OF SCREENS?... I'M BACK JUST IN TIME FOR THE COUNCIL.
I WAS SORT OF WORRIED, YOU KNOW...
OHHH, YOU SHOULDN'T HAVE BEEN! OF COURSE, THERE WAS SOME DANGER ... BUT YOU KNOW YOUR VALERIAN ALWAYS PULLS THROUGH LIKE A CHAMP!...
AHEM!... QUICKLY PLEASE, MY FRIENDS. I CANNOT WAIT TO EXPLAIN EARTH'S PEACEFUL STANCE...
LAURELINE, WAIT! WHAT IS IT? ARE YOU SULKING?...
43A
WE CAN PLAY AN ENORMOUS ROLE, I CAN FEEL IT... I'LL EXPLAIN THE CHANGE OF TACTICS TO GALAXITY LATER...
DIOL, HELP ME GET OUT OF THIS SPACESUIT. I MUST PRESENT MYSELF BEFORE THE COUNCIL IN DRESS UNIFORM...
AH! HERE'S THE GREAT HALL OF SCREENS... I SEE THAT ALL PEOPLES ARE WAITING FOR ME. WELL, THEY WON'T BE DISAPPOINTED...
LEAVE ME, MY FRIENDS. I NO LONGER NEED YOUR LOYAL HELP...
43B

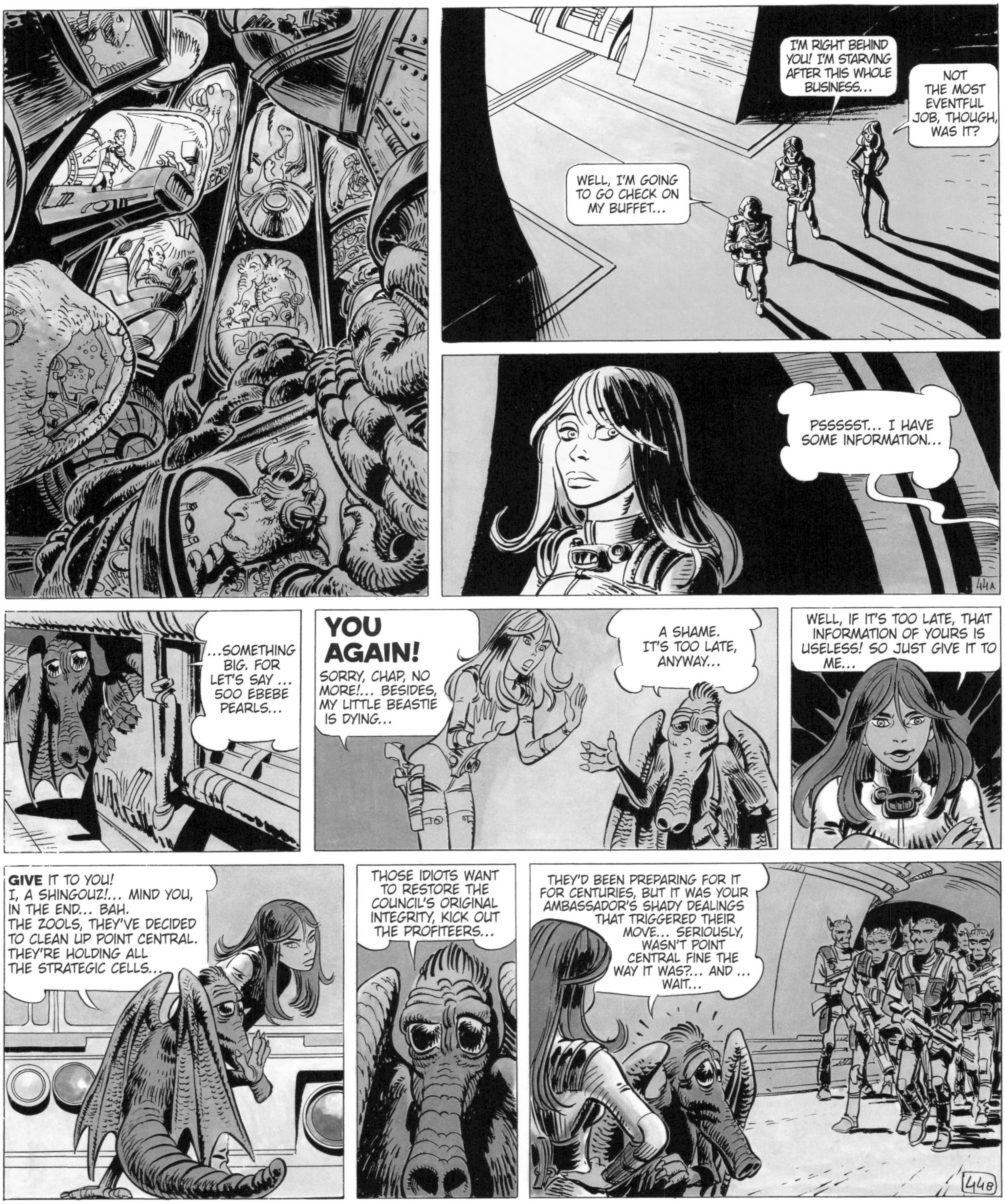
I'M RIGHT BEHIND YOU! I'M STARVING AFTER THIS WHOLE BUSINESS...
NOT THE MOST EVENTFUL JOB, THOUGH, WAS IT?
WELL, I'M GOING TO GO CHECK ON MY BUFFET...
PSSSSST... I HAVE SOME INFORMATION...
44A
...SOMETHING BIG. FOR LET'S SAY ... 500 EBEBE PEARLS...
YOU AGAIN!
SORRY, CHAP, NO MORE!... BESIDES, MY LITTLE BEASTIE IS DYING...
A SHAME. IT'S TOO LATE, ANYWAY...
WELL, IF IT'S TOO LATE, THAT INFORMATION OF YOURS IS USELESS! SO JUST GIVE IT TO ME...
GIVE IT TO YOU! I, A SHINGOUZ!... MIND YOU, IN THE END... BAH. THE ZOOLS, THEY'VE DECIDED TO CLEAN UP POINT CENTRAL. THEY'RE HOLDING ALL THE STRATEGIC CELLS...
THOSE IDIOTS WANT TO RESTORE THE COUNCIL'S ORIGINAL INTEGRITY, KICK OUT THE PROFITEERS...
THEY'D BEEN PREPARING FOR IT FOR CENTURIES, BUT IT WAS YOUR AMBASSADOR'S SHADY DEALINGS THAT TRIGGERED THEIR MOVE... SERIOUSLY, WASN'T POINT CENTRAL FINE THE WAY IT WAS?... AND ... WAIT...
44B

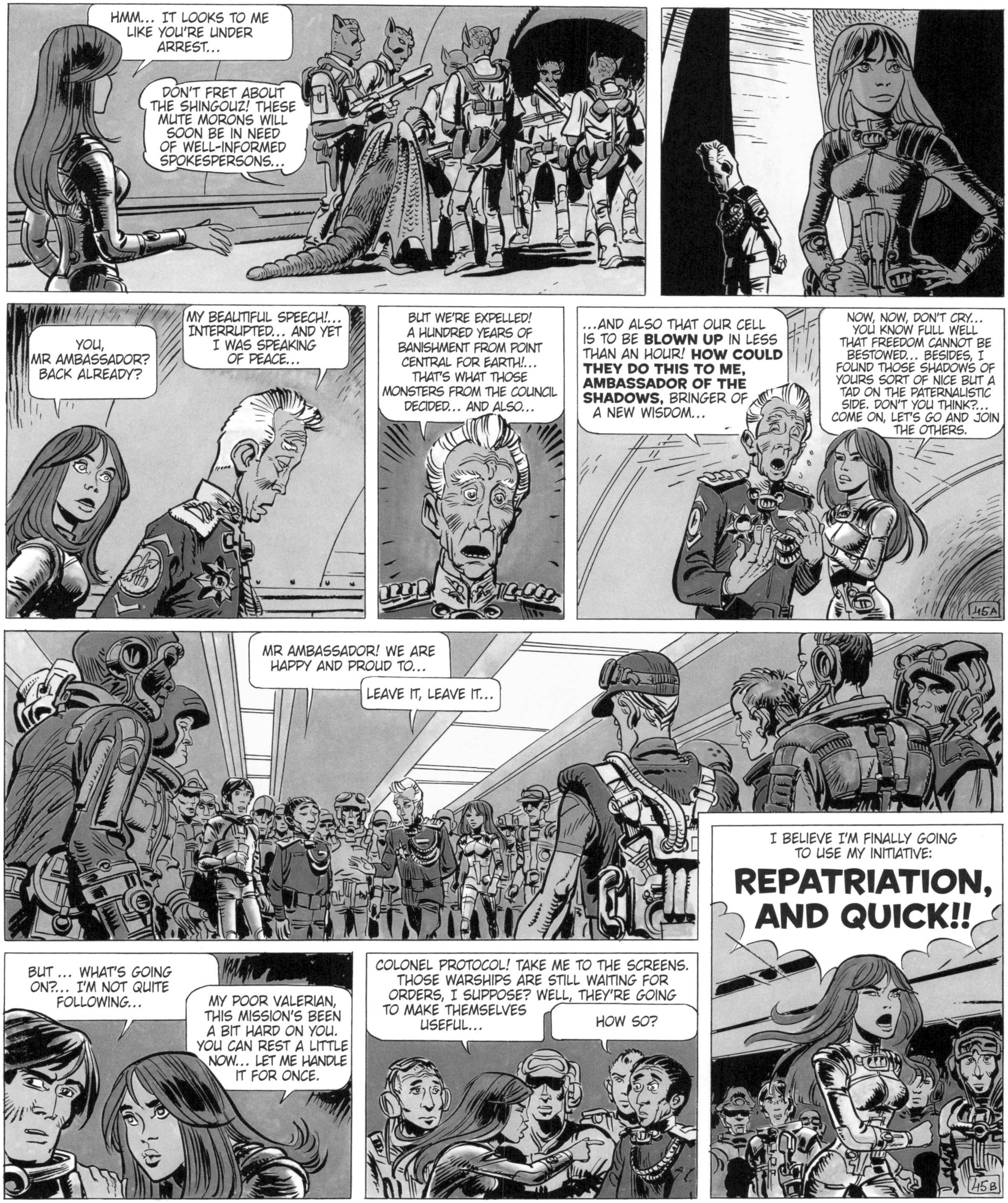
HMM... IT LOOKS TO ME LIKE YOU'RE UNDER ARREST...
DON'T FRET ABOUT THE SHINGOUZ! THESE MUTE MORONS WILL SOON BE IN NEED OF WELL-INFORMED SPOKESPERSONS...
YOU, MR AMBASSADOR? BACK ALREADY?
MY BEAUTIFUL SPEECH!... INTERRUPTED... AND YET I WAS SPEAKING OF PEACE...
BUT WE'RE EXPELLED! A HUNDRED YEARS OF BANISHMENT FROM POINT CENTRAL FOR EARTH!... THAT'S WHAT THOSE MONSTERS FROM THE COUNCIL DECIDED... AND ALSO...
...AND ALSO THAT OUR CELL IS TO BE **BLOWN UP** IN LESS THAN AN HOUR! **HOW COULD THEY DO THIS TO ME, AMBASSADOR OF THE SHADOWS,** BRINGER OF A NEW WISDOM...
NOW, NOW, DON'T CRY... YOU KNOW FULL WELL THAT FREEDOM CANNOT BE BESTOWED... BESIDES, I FOUND THOSE SHADOWS OF YOURS SORT OF NICE BUT A TAD ON THE PATERNALISTIC SIDE. DON'T YOU THINK?... COME ON, LET'S GO AND JOIN THE OTHERS.
45A
MR AMBASSADOR! WE ARE HAPPY AND PROUD TO...
LEAVE IT, LEAVE IT...
BUT ... WHAT'S GOING ON?... I'M NOT QUITE FOLLOWING...
MY POOR VALERIAN, THIS MISSION'S BEEN A BIT HARD ON YOU. YOU CAN REST A LITTLE NOW... LET ME HANDLE IT FOR ONCE.
COLONEL PROTOCOL! TAKE ME TO THE SCREENS. THOSE WARSHIPS ARE STILL WAITING FOR ORDERS, I SUPPOSE? WELL, THEY'RE GOING TO MAKE THEMSELVES USEFUL...
HOW SO?
I BELIEVE I'M FINALLY GOING TO USE MY INITIATIVE:
REPATRIATION, AND QUICK!!
45B

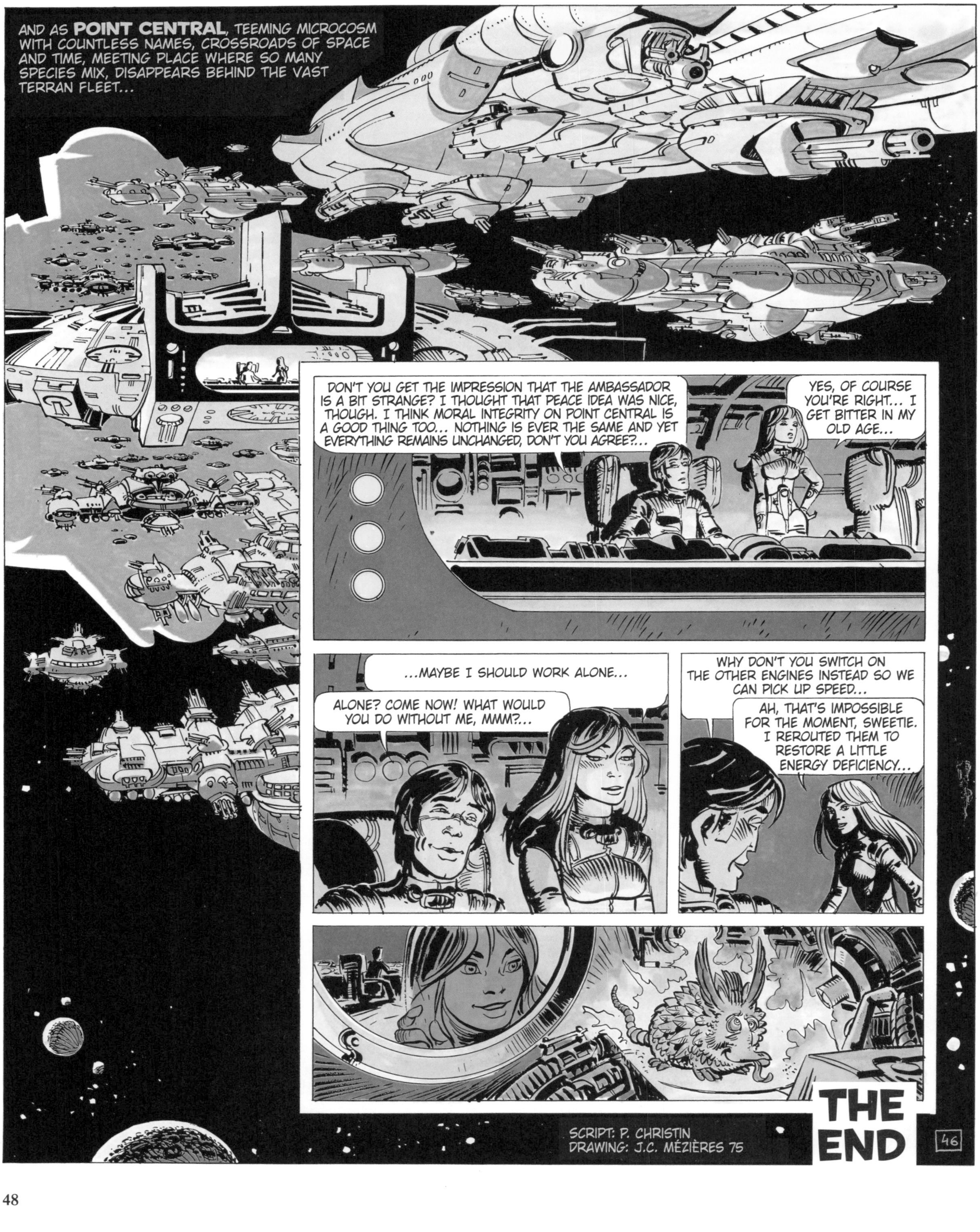
AND AS POINT CENTRAL, TEEMING MICROCOSM WITH COUNTLESS NAMES, CROSSROADS OF SPACE AND TIME, MEETING PLACE WHERE SO MANY SPECIES MIX, DISAPPEARS BEHIND THE VAST TERRAN FLEET...
DON'T YOU GET THE IMPRESSION THAT THE AMBASSADOR IS A BIT STRANGE? I THOUGHT THAT PEACE IDEA WAS NICE, THOUGH. I THINK MORAL INTEGRITY ON POINT CENTRAL IS A GOOD THING TOO... NOTHING IS EVER THE SAME AND YET EVERYTHING REMAINS UNCHANGED, DON'T YOU AGREE?...
YES, OF COURSE YOU'RE RIGHT... I GET BITTER IN MY OLD AGE...
...MAYBE I SHOULD WORK ALONE...
ALONE? COME NOW! WHAT WOULD YOU DO WITHOUT ME, MMM?...
WHY DON'T YOU SWITCH ON THE OTHER ENGINES INSTEAD SO WE CAN PICK UP SPEED...
AH, THAT'S IMPOSSIBLE FOR THE MOMENT, SWEETIE. I REROUTED THEM TO RESTORE A LITTLE ENERGY DEFICIENCY...
THE END
SCRIPT: P. CHRISTIN
DRAWING: J.C. MÉZIÈRES 75
46

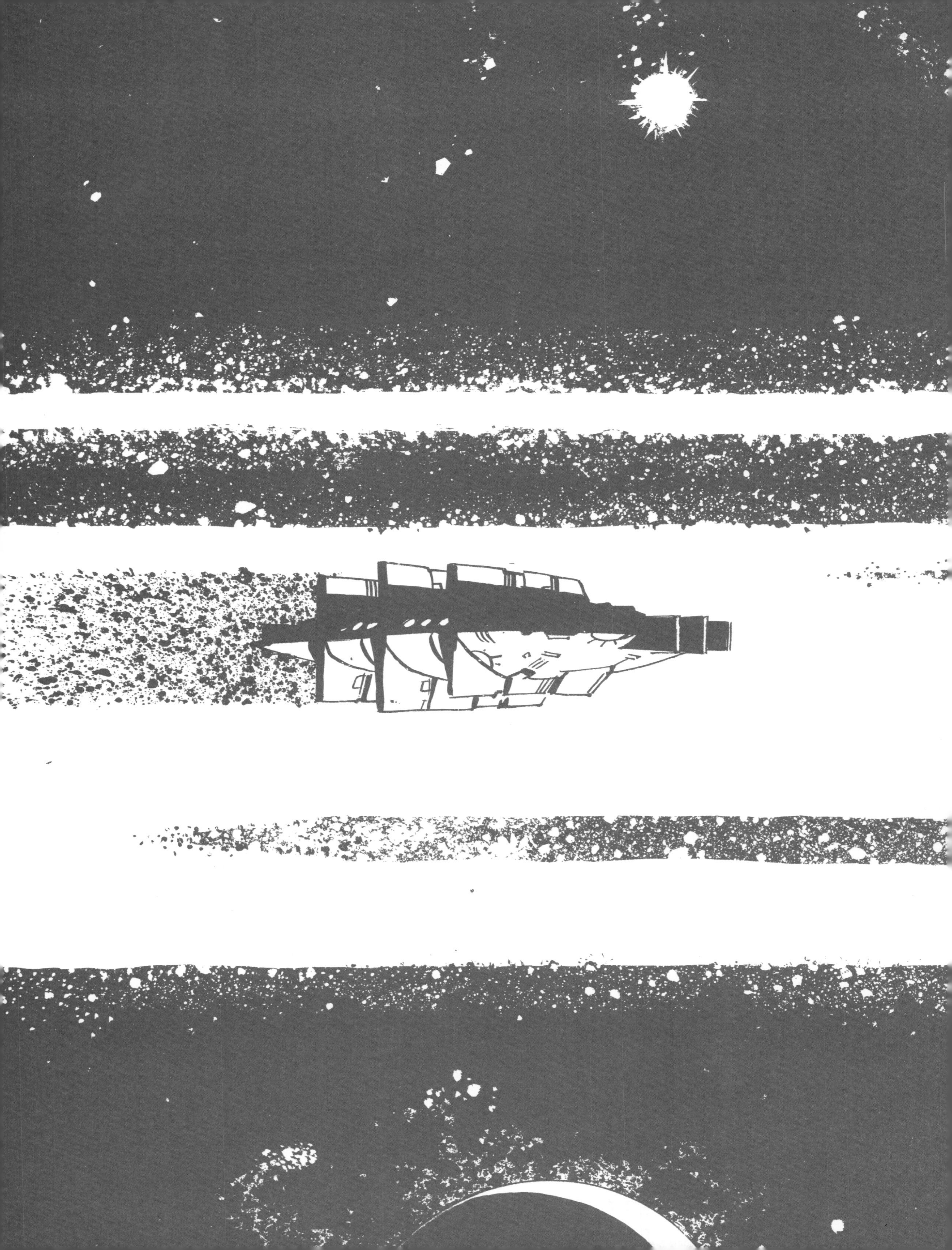